The TOLTEC
SECRET to
HAPPINESS

The TOLTEC SECRET to HAPPINESS

· · · · · · · · · · · · ·

*Creating Lasting Change
with the Power of Belief*

· · · · · · · · · · · · ·

RAY DODD

Foreword by don Miguel Ruiz, Jr.

HAMPTON ROADS

This edition first published in 2014 by
Hampton Roads Publishing Company, Inc.
Charlottesville, VA 22906
Distributed by Red Wheel/Weiser, LLC
www.redwheelweiser.com

Sign up for our newsletter and special offers by going to www.red-wheelweiser.com/newsletter/.

Cover design by *www.levanfisherdesign.com* / Barbara Fisher
Interior designed by Frame25 Productions

ISBN: 978-1-57174-704-4

Library of Congress Cataloging-in-Publication Data available upon request.

Printed on acid-free paper in the United States of America.

VG

13 12 11 10 09 08 07 06
 8 7 6 5 4 3 2 1

The paper used in this publication meets the minimum requirements of the American National Standard for Information Sciences—Permanence of Paper for Printed Library Materials Z39.48-1992 (R1997).

Your beliefs become . . . your destiny.
　—Mahatma Gandhi

CONTENTS

PART III: TOOLS

FOREWORD

My family's Toltec teachings come from a long oral tradition—accumulated wisdom shared down through the generations in the form of stories and anecdotes. One of the most beautiful elements of any tradition of knowledge is that when a student takes its lessons to heart, and begins to practice, the knowledge is transformed through experience. Through experience, knowledge becomes real wisdom and the lessons become truth in practice. And so a tradition evolves. As each generation of teachers shares its version they adapt the knowledge into new lessons for understanding life in the modern world. In this way the ancient traditions remain alive and relevant for the next group of students who are anxious for change and willing to listen.

Ray Dodd and I have the same teacher, my father, don Miguel Ruiz, MD, and we have approached what we have learned in ways as unique as the directions our lives have taken us. I first met Ray when I was in my early twenties. When he began his Toltec apprenticeship with my father, Ray was already well on his way in his own career: first in music, then in engineering, and finally in business. The result of the fusion of his paths into one is reflected in his book, *The Toltec Secret to Happiness: Create Lasting Change with the Power of Belief.*

As Ray discovered his voice, he focused his attention on the singular topic of transforming self-limiting beliefs as an effective way to achieve lasting change. The material for the book you now hold in your hands is the foundation for the Power of Belief programs he now teaches within his organization: BeliefWorks.

Why are our beliefs so powerful, and why is changing them so transforming? Whatever beliefs you have said YES to create the reality you are living today. Are you sometimes overwhelmed by stress, drama, or sadness? Do you have a belief that is holding you back from experiencing the joy and success you dream are possible? As you begin reading, set your intent to see how Ray's process of shifting limiting beliefs can help you in your own life or work. Pay close attention to these questions as you make your way through this book and I assure you, any undiscovered self-defeating beliefs you hold will be revealed to you.

It can be startling to come face-to-face with your most fearful beliefs, but it is also a gift—a rare opportunity to revitalize your health, wealth, and your most precious relationships. Take the actions suggested in the book, carefully follow the process, and something astonishing will happen; you'll change the way you see the world.

What is the Toltec Secret to Happiness? Like most secrets, it's not much of a secret at all. It's out there for all to see yet invisible to all except those who are ready hear it. The secret is simply this: *Limiting beliefs result in drama and sadness, and positive beliefs support a life filled with happiness and possibility. To eliminate self-judgment, unhappiness, conflict, and regret, you must discover the beliefs you have that are rooted in baseless fear and learn to change those beliefs.* Ray Dodd will show you how.

Ray has shared with me how much he is inspired by the belief work itself because each time he teaches it he learns something new, and the lessons of our tradition deepen for him. My father taught us that the word *Toltec* means "artist." Like all dedicated teachers Ray is a passionate artist, and now he shares his ever-evolving art with you in each of the pages in this book.

You will find an echo of my family's teachings in these pages as well, as Ray continues to contribute to the oral tradition of the Toltec. The element that makes this book a standout is Ray Dodd himself—his own struggles and his humanity are fully present in the lessons and in the voice of this book. The key for any student—or reader—of any tradition is that he or she resonates with the message of the teacher. Make no mistake about it—Ray Dodd's message comes from the voice of applied wisdom and love. *The Toltec Secret to Happiness: Create Lasting Change with the Power of Belief* is a beautiful work of art, and I am sure it will be a fundamental instrument in your path of transformation for many years to come.

With Love,

don Miguel Ruiz, Jr., author of
The Five Levels of Attachment

INTRODUCTION

B elief is Power, the power to create. You create your own reality simply by what you agree to believe. Your deepest beliefs about everything hold your attention and propel you into action, or keep you from taking action. What you believe impacts your performance at work, your attitudes about money, how you navigate through the world, and how you conduct all your relationships.

Belief colors every experience and determines how we react in any situation, yet we are often unaware of the hidden beliefs that guide us. Sometimes our beliefs hold us back from realizing our deepest desires. Oftentimes it is the long-forgotten agreements we've made with ourselves that keep us stuck, repeatedly making choices in conflict with what we say we value most.

When you come to understand the real power of belief, you'll discover you have the ability to create any point of view you choose. Learn to exercise that power and you can defeat fear-based beliefs about yourself and the world around you that keep you from the happiness and inner peace you've always desired. Harness the power of belief and you'll break through self-created boundaries you were convinced could never, ever change.

In my practice helping others change their limiting beliefs, I assist people who are motivated to face whatever is holding them back. They have already decided where they want to go; they're just not exactly sure how to get there. Traditional performance coaching focuses on what is true now, in the present moment, and what actions need to be taken to produce different results. However, mapping out strategies and taking action are only one small piece of the puzzle.

While facilitating transformation for both individuals and organizations, I have noticed that focusing on what people believe is far more powerful than trying to change behavior. Concentrating on what they believe has been vastly more effective than dissecting the stories they tell me about their problems and then working from the details. Working from the details creates managed solutions that don't last because the real problem has never been resolved. In order to effect lasting and positive change, they need to change what they believe.

The belief-change process contained in this book, born out of my own experiences and sharpened by working with hundreds of people to alter their own self-defeating beliefs, is deeply rooted in the ancient wisdom of the Toltec. In 1996 on a trip to the pyramid ruins in Teotihuacán, Mexico, I had the amazing good fortune to meet don Miguel Ruiz M.D., author of the best-selling book about the teachings of the Toltec, *The Four Agreements*. Don Miguel is a former medical doctor and teacher dedicated to carrying on his family's spiritual heritage.

Not long after the trip, I began to study with don Miguel. I went to see him on a regular basis over a period of six years and those visits began a new chapter in my life.

Prior to meeting don Miguel, I spent many years trying to find a way to heal my own unhappiness and dissatisfaction. I was always looking for something different or better. I was addicted to identifying what was wrong with everything, so I tried whatever I could think of—moving to a new place, finding a different job, starting a new relationship—all with the potential to get me what I thought I needed. I went through portions of this cycle many times, buying into the myth that I would finally be happy when I had this, or when I found that.

Having mixed results trying to change what was outside of me, I started on an inward journey that took me through many philosophies, faiths, and practices. I worked with various types of healers and read mountains of motivational and self-help books. I studied numerous spiritual traditions, had a martial arts practice in Aikido, and even spent time in a seminary.

Along the way I accumulated lots of wonderful knowledge I wholeheartedly agreed with, yet I was still struggling, frequently overpowered by unwanted emotional reactions when things didn't go the way I thought they should. At the time, I assumed simply collecting all that information would do the trick. Looking back now, I realize I wasn't living all those ideas that sounded so good to me because they were in conflict with what I really believed.

My own process of change went into high gear when I began to study with don Miguel. Nothing he taught was in conflict with what I had learned up to that point. In fact, it complemented it. I discovered the Toltec way is unique, chock-full of simple yet brilliant devices that produce extraordinary results when put into practice. I have done my best to include as many as possible in this book.

The Toltec were an ancient culture chiefly located in what is now the pyramid ruins of Teotihuacán in the high midlands of Mexico. In a tradition that dates back thousands of years and continues today, the Toltec were known throughout Mexico as men and women of knowledge. One interpretation of the word "Toltec" is "artist." They considered the manner in which you lived your life as your art; thus the Toltec way was not a religion but more accurately a way of life.

The modern Toltec view embodies many universally accepted truths adopted by bona fide faiths and spiritual traditions around the world, along with a common-sense approach to explaining what we are and how we got this way. Toltec philosophy claims that there is no way for us to change unless we have an understanding of how we create our own unique perception of the world. The Toltec description of human awareness is that the mind never rests, and one of its main purposes is to dream. Their mythology states that we are always dreaming, not only at night, but also while we are awake, and what we experience inside the dream is significantly altered by our beliefs about everything.

You are always modifying what you see, according to what you believe. What you believe produces a unique perception of the world and drives most of your thoughts, your actions, your joys, and your sorrows. It is very real, yet amazingly enough, it is only real for you and no one else.

My understanding of the true power of belief began 30 years ago when I tried to quit smoking cigarettes. Although I only smoked a few cigarettes a day, I had come to despise the habit. About that time, the government began to force cigarette manufacturers to publicize the health hazards of smoking and print warnings on the package. Even the pack of cigarettes said smoking was bad for you!

I had all the information I needed to make a decision to quit smoking, but I just couldn't stop. I would quit for a few days, buy a pack, smoke a few cigarettes, and then throw the pack away disgusted with myself. I tried everything there was on the market to help me quit smoking. I bought nicotine gum, books, tapes, and took special supplements. I even tried hypnosis, but none of it helped. Sometimes I would quit for weeks. The physical addiction to the nicotine would subside, but something much more powerful was pulling me back into the habit. My level of frustration became enormous.

One night as I was drifting off to sleep I heard an unfamiliar voice from deep within me say, *You're afraid to embrace LIFE! You can't breathe deeply without the smoke to calm your fear. You live in the shadows. You don't care whether you live or die.*

I immediately dismissed the thought as preposterous. "Of course I care. I want to live!" I said to myself. But as the days passed I started to look carefully at this thought that had risen from a level well below what I was conscious of.

You don't care whether you live or die.

The words haunted me. When I stopped denying it, something emerged from me. I became aware of a hidden memory that now existed only as a long-forgotten dream. There was a part of me that believed exactly what I had discovered. It was true and yet it had been invisible to me. That awareness was startling and yet very powerful. Maybe I believed it, but with awareness I could make a choice to no longer agree with it. The part of me that believed it was from another time in my life. Once I understood that, I stopped smoking immediately. The battle was over. It was never about smoking. It was all about what I had believed.

Whether you are aware of it or not, the entire tapestry of your life—woven together with the threads of belief—is your masterpiece. We are all Toltecs, artists of life. So whether you are interested in changing self-defeating beliefs that stand in your way, increasing your people skills by recognizing what others truly believe, or using the positive beliefs that have served you well as a springboard to the next level of personal achievement, understanding the true power of belief can be a very valuable tool.

Step by step, you will discover how to remap any belief that is an obstacle to getting the results you want, unleashing the potential for profound and enduring transformation in every part of your life.

The Toltec Secret to Happiness is divided into three sections. Part 1, "The First Dream," examines the ability we have to devise our own unique reality, or as the Toltec described it, our personal dream. It defines what belief really is, shows how our belief system was created, and describes how hidden beliefs can keep us from the happiness we dream is possible. Part 2, "The Second Dream," contains carefully designed steps for modifying any belief you want to change. Part 3, "Tools," includes a list of definitions for terms used throughout the book. Some of the terms are taken directly from the Toltec mythology, some I have modified from the original concepts, and some are my own invention.

Over the years I have noticed that what I considered a simple idea could be a maddening puzzle for my clients and students. They needed to hear it over and over again in lots of different forms before they would start to comprehend what was being said. Looking back over my own process, I did the very same thing. My teachers would repeat many times over concepts that are obvious to me now but certainly weren't then. These devices, the terms in the book, are designed to help you clearly understand the core ideas that are fundamental to create lasting and positive change.

It is awareness of the awesome force of belief that creates possibility. Possibility limited only by what you can imagine. Positive belief anchored in respect, love, integrity, and self-acceptance provides you, the artist, with a new brush that makes bold strokes. It is time to create the life you've only dreamed of. But to do this you must be ready. Ready to change what you believe!

PART ONE

THE FIRST DREAM

◆ ◆ ◆ ◆ ◆ ◆ ◆ ◆ ◆ ◆ ◆ ◆

We don't see things as they are, we see things as we are.
—Anaïs Nin

CHAPTER 1

THE FABRIC OF BELIEF

A belief is a dream, a simulated reality shaped by your most pivotal experiences and what you have decided those experiences mean. A conviction that exists beyond language, belief projects its point of view onto all that you perceive, distorting what is.

If you want to change your life—Right Now—there is nothing more powerful than changing what you believe!

Belief creates your personal reality: a unique world view where often what is true is true only for you. What I am referring to are not political beliefs or beliefs about religion, but the unseen agreements you made long ago that impact every word you say, every thought you think, and every action you take. The voice of those agreements is the conversation you hear chattering in your mind—proclaiming how things are, describing what you know, telling you about everything you believe.

Your interpretation of life through your filter of beliefs alters what you perceive. Imagine you and I are looking at a dog. If you remember your high school biology, the light reflecting off the dog enters the retina in your eye and through a series of biochemical reactions, receptors process what you see, sending an electrical impulse to the brain and creating an image in your mind. The image is raw data. What you actually take in is modified by how you interpret the data.

We project what we believe onto whatever we are experiencing. The process is similar to the way a movie projector works. Light passes through a moving film and the images on the film are projected onto a screen through a lens. If the lens isn't clean the images are distorted. In the same way, your beliefs coat the lens of your awareness; and when light reflects off what you see, your beliefs alter what you perceive inside your mind.

What you observe is not actual but virtual. If I love dogs and you are afraid of dogs, we are each going to have a different experience. What you see and feel and what I see and feel are not exactly the same even though we are looking at the same dog. In a similar way, if a college art class is drawing a human model, the students don't all draw the same thing in the same way. Granted, some of this is because not everyone has the same level of skill or technique, but more importantly, the artists are expressing what they see inside their own virtual reality.

Most of the time we don't have any direct contact with what we observe at all. Unless we are tasting something, or feeling the texture and temperature by touching it, our perception is derived largely from the image in our mind and the sounds we hear.

No one has a pure perception of the world they encounter moment to moment because we alter the information received by the senses based on past experiences and our agreements about those experiences. An example: If I invite you to dinner at my mother's house and she serves us my favorite dish, what you taste will likely be different from what I taste. Similarly, if you invite me to a concert where they are performing music you're familiar with, but I've never heard before, my experience is not going to be the same as yours.

To make matters worse, we distort the already altered version of reality presented to us by other people. To illustrate, let's say you are my friend. You know me and we have talked many times. You go to a party and get into a conversation with a man you've never met before. You tell the man about me but you don't give him my name. My sister goes to the same party and talks to the same man about me but also does not mention my name. By chance the next day my mother runs into the very same man in the supermarket and while they are waiting in the checkout line, she starts to tell him about me, her son. It is likely this man will think he was told about three different people because what he heard was how I existed in each of their minds. What he experienced was their perception of me through the lens of their judgments, opinions, and beliefs.

The typical understanding of belief is that it is a product of the mind, produced by our reason. Something is true because we think it is true. We are under the impression that what we think we believe is actually what we believe. However, what we *think* we believe is often just an opinion. Opinions are not beliefs but the application of all the accumulated knowledge we have agreed to and our relentless defense of those agreements. Belief is so much more than what we think is true. The origin of belief is not words but experience, the emotion that arises from that experience, and the evolution of what we perceive that experience to mean.

Is it possible to develop a belief without language, without thinking about it? Of course it is! A toddler that has been scratched by a cat develops an instant belief about cats (watch out!) without understanding words.

From the Toltec perspective, everything we believe about ourselves, and everything we have decided we know about our world is filled with illusions fabricated by the dreaming mind.

So, consider a broader definition for the word "belief."

A belief is a dream, a simulated reality shaped by your most pivotal experiences and what you have decided those experiences mean. A conviction that exists beyond language, belief projects its point of view onto all that you perceive, distorting what is.

What you believe is what you have no doubt about. Let's say you need to run an errand and you decide to drive your car to get there. You leave your house, walk out to the car, open the car with your keys, get in, put the key in the ignition, start the car, and begin to drive away. For most people, this whole sequence is pretty routine. You don't think much about it. You aren't considering how a key works in a lock or how the motor of a car operates after you turn the key. You don't consider it because you've done it many times, and you don't have any doubt about what will happen. It's not conscious, it's automatic. You believe it works. You believe it works because that is where you have invested your faith.

Where your faith is invested is powerful and very difficult to change just by changing your thinking. As an example, according to psychologists the greatest fear people have is not of dying but of speaking in front of other people. Many people have stage fright and so one way to overcome this fear is to take a public speaking course. A course like that can be helpful, but what it really does is help manage fear. When they step out onto the stage, even after they've finished the course, there is often still something trying to overpower all the affirmations, techniques, and good intentions. That something is what they believe about themselves.

Many times our most deeply held beliefs are invisible to us. We think we know what we believe, but maybe we really don't. Ask yourself: What do I believe about money? What do I believe about my work? What do I really believe about God, love, family, or the immense world around me? You can probably come up with some pretty good answers, but are they true? Suppose you tell everyone that you believe in being kind, considerate, and loving. What happens when someone doesn't act kind, considerate, and loving towards you? How do you feel when someone doesn't act kind or considerate towards someone you care about? When you are driving your car and another driver does something you don't like, is your reaction in conflict with what you told everyone you believed?

Belief can be so powerful that it controls your entire body. Just look in the mirror when you are upset or stressed.

Look at your face and how you are standing—your posture. Notice whether your breathing is deep or shallow. Belief affects our biological systems too. There is much written about how fear, stress, and negative thinking can cause dis-ease in the human body. There is also mountains of evidence about how love, positive thought, laughter, and touch aid in the healing of the same diseases.

Because belief lives below the level of ordinary awareness, you don't notice the agreements you made long ago. What you notice is the emotional point of view of the belief. When you are triggered by a stressful situation, what you're really aware of is being overwhelmed by an emotion. Even if you have learned to hold back your words, your reaction is far more powerful than any thought you might have about how you should or shouldn't act. It's a runaway train and you're not in control. In those moments, forcing yourself to behave in a way you think is acceptable can be like trying to strap down the lid on the pot so the water doesn't boil over while the flame underneath is turned all the way up.

Real transformation of the belief system cannot be accomplished simply by deciding to believe something else, reciting affirmations, or collecting more information. Have you ever been to a seminar, come back all fired up with lots of good information and the best intentions. only to find months later that not much has really changed? You learn to talk the talk, but you can't seem to walk the walk. The change doesn't last because what really drives behavior is belief. Real transformation of your beliefs comes from engaging the totality of what you are, not just your mind.

You are so much more than intellect and reason. You are vastly more than your thinking. You are this human body with the senses of touch, sight, hearing, taste, and smell. You are instinct and intuition. You are a feeling being with emotions. You are spirit imbued with the force of LIFE—aware—and through your perception, *a dreamer.*

For years, I had a very hard time understanding the Toltec perspective that we are always dreaming. I thought it meant nothing was real. That's not exactly true. What it means is that we don't accurately experience what is in front of us, but perceive instead a virtual image altered by the activity of the dreaming mind. How we interpret what we experience is dramatically influenced by the structure of our beliefs.

Our personal dream, our individual simulated reality, is the solid and familiar story we exist in. It becomes so familiar that we no longer notice it. Only when something drastic happens to suspend it—like an accident, illness, sudden loss, or other tragedy—do we get a glimpse of the world without our usual filters. In those moments, the mirage evaporates and we begin to see the limitless possibilities available by changing what we believe.

Years ago, after a trip into the interior of Mexico, I came down with malaria. I was very sick with a high fever. Six weeks later, I finally started to get better, but I was still weak and had lost a lot of weight.

Some friends of mine took me out for a walk in a local mountain park. They thought it would do me good to get outside into the fresh spring air. We walked for a short way and then I decided we should turn back because

I was getting tired. Just as we turned around to go back, we passed a man and a woman walking the other way. The man called my name. He said, "Ray?" I turned around and looked at him. He seemed pleasant but I didn't recognize him. I began to walk away. "Ray?" he said again. I looked harder. I had a warm feeling looking at him. His face was bathed in the late afternoon light and seemed soft, like the effect you get when you spread gel on a camera lens. Still, I couldn't recall his face and so I started to walk down the hill. He called out loudly, "Ray!" I looked back at him and struggled to place him. I stared directly at him for what seemed to me to be a very long time. All of a sudden, I heard a popping sound as if something that had been stuck released, and there was a return to a more familiar feeling.

I could now see this was Steve, a man I'd known for several years. Steve worked at the same company I did. I liked him and thought he was immensely intelligent, but we would often disagree because I thought he had a habit of rushing into things with way more enthusiasm than planning. Like just about everyone else in my life I had a judgment about him. My long illness, however, had severely diminished my attachment to just about everything—my possessions, my personal history, and my judgments. Much of what I had deemed serious and important was no longer even worth considering. I just didn't have the energy to maintain being right. Part of my world before I became sick was Steve; the way I judged him, defined him, and even gossiped about him. Because the illness had largely dissolved that, I saw him in a very different way. So different in fact I could not even recognize him!

CHAPTER 2

THE PATH TO NOW

What you are experiencing in this very moment is the
culmination of everything you have agreed to believe.

In order to change any of the beliefs that are holding you
back from creating the life you want, it's important to
understand how they were formed and what got you to
this point.

For many years behavioral scientists have studied
human infants to determine what their experience is and
how they develop. Very small children can't express in words
what is happening to them, so all we can do is observe. Just
looking at a baby you can see that their eyes act like the
lens of a video camera. Their attention shifts from moment
to moment. They focus on whatever is enchanting, interesting, and catches their eye. They stare at it until it holds
no more fascination and then move their attention to
something else. They seem to gravitate towards what gives
them pleasure and move away from what is confusing or
doesn't feel good. What they perceive, what channels of

communication they establish, and what they experience are determined solely by where they focus their attention.

Babies and toddlers are little human beings without language. They don't possess the ability to express to others in words what they are experiencing. They observe the world through the five physical senses and their intuitive sense of feeling. How things feel is a big part of how they perceive and process their surroundings. Unlike adults, who use words to describe what they feel, babies don't have language to interpret the emotion, yet their emotional awareness carries terabytes of information about the essence of what is happening moment to moment.

A friend of mine was in the process of deciding whether she and her husband would get a divorce. They were still living together, but emotionally they had already separated. They had a two-year-old son who was walking but had not yet begun to speak. Her son would make them sit down on the couch and insist they hold hands. Although he didn't have the ability to understand the words they were speaking, he could sense exactly what was going on between them. It didn't feel good, so he took action to make it different.

Little children exist in a kind of paradise. They have the capacity to perceive what is without a lot of distortion, unlike the adults who interpret everything through their experiences. Little children notice the essence of things guided by the truth of their emotions. Emotions never lie. They advise impeccably based on how it feels.

These little humans are free to be who they are. Sometimes they hurt and sometimes they are afraid, but they live in the present moment with a great capacity to enjoy life—to play, to be endlessly curious, and to love.

As adults, we need to be able to communicate with our children. We want to give instructions, ask questions, and when necessary, take control. Parents have a basic understanding of their small children through a series of nonverbal clues, but eventually they have to establish a better channel of communication. In order to successfully communicate, children need to learn the code. They need to learn language—an agreement about what the sounds mean. Once the code is understood, information can be given.

The passing of any information requires the focus of your awareness. The focus of your awareness is your attention. You receive pictures, sounds, feelings, and words from any situation through your attention. To learn anything you have to pay attention, and . . . you have to agree.

By capturing our attention and teaching us the code, the adults in our lives pass on to us their personal view of the world. They teach us what everything is. They tell us their opinions about everybody and what they think of themselves. They tell us what we are, and maybe more importantly, what we are not. It's like downloading a program onto a computer. Unfortunately, if it is a view of the world infected with irrational fears, it acts like a virus in the program, eventually creating beliefs anchored in the very same fears.

One of my clients told me a story about his fear of heights. For as long as he could remember, he had been afraid of ledges, cliffs, and stairs to high places. In working toward his belief about this, he remembered that as a kid his mother had shrieked at him when he got too close to the edge of a ravine, stood on a wall, or tried to climb a tree. "David!" she would yell. "Be careful! Look out!" His fear was her fear of heights, and she had infected him with it.

By hooking our attention the adults create a channel of communication and inoculate us by way of the broadcast that comes through the channel. Through our attention there is a transmission with each person—a broadcast of his or her personal dream in that moment. The information we receive is far more than just words. Like a movie it has sound, color, movement, emotional tension, ambience, and texture. The channel of communication is like two movie projectors with images, sounds, and meaning riding the light back and forth between the attention of the human beings.

Each concept the adults tell us about, each opinion they share is the way they reveal their personal dream. What they are sharing is their perception of the world altered by their own unique filter of beliefs. These lessons come in many different forms, but when our attention is captivated an impression is made. This process of capturing our attention for the first time creates our initial dream of how the world is. Seizing our attention for the first time is what the Toltec called "The Dream of the First Attention" or for simplicity what I will call in this book: The First Dream.

Over time and through repetition these impressions become alive in your mind, but only when you agree to whatever idea, point of view, or opinion is presented. All genuine communication is by agreement. If you and I were to cook a meal together, for example, we would need to have a basic agreement about the function and name for things in a kitchen. For a solid channel of communication to be opened we have to agree on an interpretation of the raw data reaching us as light rays and sound waves. Each of us modifies what we perceive, creating our own individual virtual reality, so opening a complete channel of communication requires a similar interpretation, a shared distortion, if you will.

For little children acceptance of this distortion is not by choice but a requirement for survival. As a child, you had very little choice. Your name, the language you speak, where you lived, and where you went to school were all choices you had no say in. Maybe the adults that raised you even decided what you were supposed to believe, but in order for any of their opinions, points of view, or beliefs to begin to take hold, you still had to agree.

To illustrate this, imagine a small boy playing in his parents' house. His mother has left him alone while she is working in another part of the house. He finds some big colorful markers and starts drawing on the wall. He's totally absorbed in what he is doing and having a great time. He has a big grin on his face. Drawing pictures on the wall is pure pleasure for him.

Suddenly his mother comes back into the room. She sees him, comes up behind him, and smacks him on the bottom, yelling, "I don't have time for this! You make me so mad! You're ruining my life! If it weren't for you I could have a life!" Her anger shakes him out of his child-dream. His attention is now hooked by her rage. His emotion is overwhelming, yet absolutely authentic. It hurts because what he is experiencing is not a mother's unconditional love but the gale force of her fear.

Suppose in his own way the little boy agrees with what she has said. Maybe he thinks, "She doesn't want me anymore because I'm ruining her life." As a reaction to the emotion he felt and his new agreement, he makes a decision about what happened and that becomes his story. Maybe he is convinced that being high-spirited and creative is not okay. Perhaps he decides he will run away and then she will be better off, or that he's responsible for her anger and if he wants her to love him again, he has to be different.

As the years go by the pattern continues. His mom is constantly overwhelmed, routinely reacting in frustration to what is normal when you have children around the house. He never knows what to expect. She slams doors, yells, and even breaks things when he doesn't act the way she wants him to. He feels trapped with nowhere to go. Each time it happens he feels a similar emotion and makes more and more decisions. *I won't do what you tell me to. If you don't like me, then I don't like you. I can't wait to get out of here.*

A belief grows stronger through reinforcement and repetition. Incidents repeated over and over again in many different forms all carrying the same general message become very strong beliefs. Once they take hold, they have a life of their own. Although they start out as the result of someone else's opinion, we interpret what we experience in our own way and make up a story to support our interpretation. It becomes the story of our life. Not a story with a beginning, middle, and an end but the way we, the storyteller, describe everything and everyone in our life. It's a story based on what we have agreed to believe about everything that has happened to us.

The stories we make up to support our interpretation of what happened, have a distinct emotional point of view. And, the story corrupts what we remember. Now when something happens that is in any way similar to what is in our memory, the belief beneath it rises to the surface, appearing first as a familiar emotion.

Imagine the little boy is now a young man. He has a job and he tries his best to make a good impression. He works hard and wants everyone to notice he is doing a good job.

One afternoon at work, his boss comes in suddenly and catches him joking around with some of his friends. She tells them they need to get back to work or they are all going to be in trouble. She says something sarcastic and leaves quickly, slamming the door. The whole scene upsets him. There is a familiar emotional surge. His mind starts racing. *It's not fair. We weren't doing anything wrong. Who does she think she is? I'll start looking for another job tomorrow.*

Something deep and invisible has been touched. His strategy to be accepted, the mask he shows everyone at work, is penetrated. The belief that he is not wanted and the memory of an unpredictable parent come alive and are now in full control of his attention. The belief is expressing itself through how he interprets the situation, his emotions, and the conversation he is having in his mind defending his point of view.

The adults who captured our attention for the first time, creating our initial dream of the world, were only passing on what they learned from the adults when they were children. The same thing happened to all of our friends, and so as children we are influenced not only by our own inner circle of adults, but by the circle of adults around our playmates and schoolmates as well.

This dynamic is neither good nor bad. It's how knowledge, traditions, and legacies are passed down from generation to generation. Sometimes, however, what gets transmitted hobbles us. As little children, we live in a world full of wonderment, possibility, and imagination. Because we have our integrity intact, we believe *I Am* and *I Can*. We believe things like: *I am wanted, the world is beautiful, I am loved, I can do anything I choose* . . . and so on. Often the grown-ups introduce an entirely different outlook. An outlook based in fear.

The adults are stronger, bigger, and have the power. Assaulted by an outlook strangled with unreasonable fears, beyond good parenting and sound discipline, we know something is terribly wrong. We rebel. We say "No!" Eventually those in charge wear us down. They teach us self-judgment, the primary tool of domestication. Our little village has been under siege for days, months, maybe even years. At some point we capitulate, overpowered and outmaneuvered. Defeated, we come out of the gates waving the white flag and declare, "I surrender. I give up. I agree." *I Can* becomes *I Can Not*. *I AM* becomes *I Am Not*.

This is the path to now. What you are experiencing in this very moment is the culmination of everything you have agreed to believe. As the adults capture our attention and teach us the code—language—they open channels of communication into their own personal dream. We are slowly pulled from paradise. In the construction of The First Dream we make the long journey from operating with the intelligence of what we feel to developing a thinking mind filled with words. In our march towards physical maturity, we lose the ability to notice the essence of the present moment and become dominated by the intellect and reason. Over time each opinion, each idea, each belief makes an impression but only if we agree. If the adults in charge domesticate us under the boot of their fear, we will recycle many of their views even if we outwardly reject them. At a certain point we become overpowered by a runaway mind and frequent emotional reactions. At this juncture, our beliefs are in complete control of our attention.

In The First Dream, your beliefs control your attention.

Of course, not every belief created on the path to now is limiting, nor is every limiting belief a barrier to achievement. In the fabrication of The First Dream many wonderful and positive things happen that can support us later in creating a life we love. Everyone has memories of joyful encounters, wise teachings, and gifts of compassion that helped them bloom. Identifying the core beliefs that enhance your life is important, yet to exact real and lasting change it is necessary to recognize any belief that is keeping you from realizing the happiness and success you want. By focusing your attention for a second time, with awareness, you can create a whole new dream of life—an extraordinary life—this time carefully choosing what you want to believe.

CHAPTER 3

THE ISLAND OF WHAT YOU KNOW

The Island of What You Know is the result of what you've agreed to and where you have invested your faith. It is the container of "me" bounded by what you believe.

Imagine the beginning of a movie. The camera starts with a panoramic view of the town. The view narrows to a particular part of town, down a street, and then finally to a specific house. In the scene, you are introduced to what is happening in front of the house. The eye of the camera goes into the house, up the stairs, and begins to pan around the room until it stops on the character that is of the most interest in the story. The main character. As you follow the viewpoint presented by the camera, you get introduced to the environment the main character lives in and to all the other characters in the story. You see what's happening around them, who is in their lives each day, what is working for them, and what they are struggling with. Through this window into their world, you begin to understand what's going on. Once you understand what's happening, you can relate to them and get involved in the story.

You live in your own world just like the main character in the movie. Everyone you have ever met, everywhere you have ever lived, all the jobs you have ever had, all the trips you have been on, all the memorable events (good and bad)—everything that has ever happened to you constitutes the Island of What You Know. Your personal island is constructed of your beliefs, your opinions, other people's opinions, your experiences, and all your accumulated knowledge.

We interpret what we experience moment to moment using everything on our island. One of the reasons we do this is safety. The Island of What You Know is really an island of safety. We need to explain things so they fit within the boundaries of the Island. If something is unexplainable then it exists outside the limits of the Island and is unknown.

In the great Age of Discovery when explorers like Columbus and Magellan roamed uncharted seas, the ancient mapmakers had a device for dealing with the limits of their knowledge: They drew an edge to the world and a boundless sea beyond. Some showed it filled with huge whirlpools and imaginary creatures while others just wrote, "Here there be dragons."

We are often afraid of what is beyond the borders of what we know. If by chance we encounter it, we may dismiss it, make assumptions about it, pass judgment on it, or even pretend it doesn't exist. It takes courage to explore the unknown, expand our boundaries, and then encompass what we discover as known.

You normally assess what you see based on the Island of What You Know. You focus in tightly and if what is before you has never been on your Island, you tend not to see it. There was a famous experiment by anthropologists in the 1920s with the Me'en people, a primitive tribe located in Ethiopia. Up to that point, they had no exposure to modern civilization. When photographs of people and animals were shown to them, they felt the paper, tasted it and sniffed it, yet they were unable to recognize the two-dimensional images in the pictures.

Even a giant leap of technology fueled by genius can be severely limited by the boundaries of the Island. Alexander Graham Bell, inventor of the telephone, envisioned his creation as a way to deliver news and classical music to subscribers. Only after being presented with mounds of evidence, over a long period of time, could Bell be convinced that people were actually using his device to talk to each other.

What is on your Island is your truth, yet very often it is only true for you. The Island of What You Know is the result of what you've agreed to and where you have invested your faith. It is the container of "me" bounded by what you believe.

In the construction of The First Dream the adults captured our attention, taught us language, and opened channels of communication into their own personal dream by sharing their knowledge and opinions about everything. Much of what is on our Island is actually other people's opinions about how things are and how we are.

We develop opinions because we are uncomfortable not knowing. We like things explained and sewn up into a nice little package. We feel unsafe not knowing what will happen next. Who's going to do what. Who might say what. Who might act this way and who's going to act that way. In order to make something known we fill in the blanks and make a habit of assuming things. We put a lot of energy into creating assumptions that make us feel safe. We feel better saying, "That's how it is," or "This is what will happen," even if it isn't completely true.

In dealing with the unknown, people often turn to superstition. Superstitions create tremendous barriers to awareness because they superimpose explanations and assumptions that aren't true over what is. From the beginning of human history people have used props and invented answers steeped in superstition because of their fear of saying, "I don't know."

With the fall of Roman civilization in the fifth century, Europe plunged into a Dark Age of superstition. In dealing with something as powerful and unpredictable as nature, humans at that time needed to impose a system that provided answers to what they were seeing. In medieval Europe the order of the universe was explained as: The Sun revolves around the Earth, the Earth is flat, if you venture out too far you'll fall off. What was true then is still true now—we see what we want to see according to what we believe.

Because of our insatiable need to know, we develop expectations. An expectation is an assumption about what is *supposed* to happen. Unfortunately, expectation is the mother of crisis. When something doesn't happen as expected, it often ignites a crisis.

An example: Let's say you are going to the airport to take a trip on an airplane. You have made the journey before. You know the way, about how long it takes to get there, and where to park. You are familiar with the routine once you get into the airport with tickets, security, and boarding. You have a pretty good idea what to expect. This time however, on the way into the airport, your car suddenly stops working and you have to pull over on the side of the road. You are going to miss your plane!

In a situation like having a car breakdown, most of us struggle with the uncertainty of what might happen next. We get distressed because things are not going as expected. In a crisis, when our expectations fail us, we are always off the Island of What We Know.

The desire to put everything within the borders of our Island is very strong. This is why we make assumptions. We need to know what will happen if we do this or if we do that. We second-guess. We predict. We assume our perception is the extent of possibility and that others see things the way we do. Because of past history we assume we know what people will do, how they will react, and what they will probably say.

When we meet someone for the first time we ask, "What do you do for a living?" We guess their age, look at their clothes, and listen to how they talk. If we can't collect enough information we tend to assume a lot about them. We need to define the people we don't know and place them within the boundaries of what we do know. We need to create an assessment, an interpretation, so they become known. Only then can we form an opinion and a description that makes sense.

Years ago I was traveling with a couple in Italy, and we went to a reservation center on the outskirts of Venice. This center booked rooms for many of the hotels inside the town. We were looking for some moderately priced rooms and had the reservation person call a hotel to see if they had a vacancy. The hotel clerk put the reservation person on hold. Immediately my traveling companions started to talk nervously about what we would do if a moderately priced room was not available. Maybe we would need to book an expensive four-star hotel room! There was a lot of heated discussion around it. As soon as the hotel put the reservation clerk on hold, the couple went into the unknown. They were unable to wait and see what might happen next. They had to make a plan. Discuss. Argue. Project an outcome by assuming things. That way they felt better because they were back on their Island.

The need to place everything on the Island of What You Know is very powerful. Have you ever been traveling, awakened in a strange place, and for just a moment not known where you were? It can be very unsettling. Nothing makes sense. We don't feel right until we know what is behind every door. We need to make everything solid. Rock solid.

As the structure of the Island begins to take form, we demand clarity. We need to know, but as we seek more and more information the knowledge begins to rule us. All that information becomes an Interpreter telling us what is going on right in front of our eyes. The runaway chatter of the mind has our attention most of the time. Knowledge, expressing itself through the non-stop voice in our head, becomes like God—all knowing and all seeing.

There is a wonderful word that comes from Nahuatl, a language spoken by the people of Teotihuacán, the Toltec and the Aztecs. *Mitote* (me-toe-tay). Now a common term used in modern Mexican culture, *Mitote* refers to a noisy party, a riot, a clamor. Don Miguel used the word *Mitote* to describe our incessant internal dialog: the cacophony of characters in your head; a riot of opinions; a thousand voices in the marketplace all talking but none listening.

Our entire story—an echo of the Mitote—keeps us safe. Safe from whatever we are afraid of. Even if we are miserable, even if our Island is the Island of Hell, it explains everything. We know who we are, and what we can and cannot do. We make up a story about how everything is, and become so invested in our story we will defend it at any cost. We collect evidence so we can easily justify our stories. Why this is possible and that is impossible. Why I get along with him and why I can't get along with her. Why this will work and that will never work. Why things always end up this way. We describe ourselves with stories. "I have a temper." "I'm not a morning person." "I've always been this way." It's familiar. We are attached to our story on the Island of What We Know. It's our image and identity. It's "me." It's "my life." It's "who I am." We make up a story so everything fits in its box, carefully laid next to all the boxes on the Island.

It takes a great deal of energy to hold together the Island of What You Know. When I was in grade school, I remember playing with my friends in the woods near the school and coming upon the remains of an old asphalt road. The plants growing underneath it had cracked it, buckled it, and heaved it over the years. Moisture, the forest plants, and the freezing and thawing of the earth had reclaimed it back to nature. As long as the road, a man-made structure, received attention through regular maintenance, the road had remained a road. When the energy of human attention was withdrawn, natural forces took over and the road disintegrated. Its existence was dependent on continual patching, regularly reinforcing the structure.

Your whole framework, the Island of What You Know, is very similar to that. It is constructed of what you believe—what you have invested your faith in. You pour lots of energy into it daily, maintaining it and grooming it. The big Mitote in your mind that plans, worries, schemes, discusses and argues, works day and night fortifying the Island of What You Know.

We tend the Island each day with total dedication, taking complete responsibility for its care. There is a moment when we are just waking up, riding an edge between two worlds—the asleep world and the everyday awake world. As soon as we are fully awake, we begin to remember who we are, what we are, and where we are. Our familiar mind-chatter kicks in and off we go! All at once, we are deeply immersed in our current description of the world. Every morning we awaken from our nightly sleep and start the motor of the mind, resurrecting our personal Island.

You invest an enormous amount of energy assuming things and concocting descriptions that may or may not be true. The obsession to interpret and define everything severely constrains your ability to perceive what is really happening in each moment. On the Island of What You Know, you limit your nearly limitless possibilities. In the endless pursuit of knowledge so you can be in control and feel safe, you become what you study and the knowledge controls you. The Island of What You Know is a container of your own making and like water, you take the form of the container.

What would happen if you suddenly stepped off your Island? What would happen if you suspended your interpretation of everything, even for just one moment, allowing yourself to observe the world without your habitual lens of belief? What you might see is a new world of possibility without the story. Your story.

In the movie *The Truman Show*, the main character grows up in a made-up world that is actually a television stage. In the film, his life has been broadcast as a TV show every day since he was born. He is now grown up, married, and lives on a fake island in a town full of actors. He has no knowledge of this and believes he is living a normal life until a series of technical flaws begins to dispel the illusion. He starts to question what is authentic. At the movie's climax, he is in complete conflict with what he once accepted as true and tries to escape by taking a sailboat out onto the ocean. Instead of finding a way out, he runs into a theatrical backdrop painted to look like the horizon on the ocean. At first he is confused, but as his disbelief of what he is witnessing begins to evaporate, he clearly sees the construct of his world. He finds a door in the backdrop, opens it, and for the first time in his life sees the world that lies beyond the boundary of the enormous television stage. In that moment he steps off his Island to a new and yet unknown freedom.

We generally accept the reality of the world with which we are presented. We become fashioned by the culture we live in and by the language we speak. We think we are what we think. We live on our own personal mesa bounded by our beliefs, agreements, and opinions.

If you really want to change what you believe, venture off the Island of What You Know. By stepping off your island you may discover a whole other world. A world of mind-altering possibility.

Stepping off the Island of What You Know requires two things. The first one is awareness. Awareness of what is on your Island. This first step is about clearly seeing the boundaries created by what you believe about yourself and everything around you. Pay attention to what you keep saying to yourself about yourself. When you speak about yourself to others, what do you say? How do you introduce yourself? What do you keep saying to other people about your past, your future, money, work, or love? Become aware of what's in your life that you identify with, what you defend, what you are attached to, and what really scares you when you consider giving it up.

The second requirement for stepping off the Island of What You Know is letting go of always needing to know— always needing to know why. Do you have a habit of assuming things? When the unexpected happens, how do you respond? Try, even for just a moment, giving up your expectations about how everything is supposed to be. Can you really be sure how people will act or in what direction things might go? Can you be absolutely certain what might happen next? Experiment with letting go of the addiction to filling in the blanks and allow your experience to unfold in front of you.

The Island of What You Know is often constructed for survival. Letting go of tight-fisted control can be a scary thing. All of a sudden the ground beneath your feet isn't as solid as you thought it was. To see life as it is, you have to step away from what you believe it is or you just won't see it. To begin, venture off the Island of What You Know.

CHAPTER 4

FAITH AND THE BROKEN HEART

Recognizing the beliefs born of the broken heart and
changing the decisions you made so long ago begin a
new journey, releasing your passion and true power.

As time passes we adopt the lessons of The First Dream
and build our own life. What was once other people's
construction of reality becomes the foundation of our own
unique structure. We redecorate—painting it the colors
we like, buying curtains and putting in new carpet. From
the dream that was passed on to us we develop our own
opinions and points of view. We continually re-form and
reinforce our personal Island until it defines the boundaries
of "me."

The fabrication of the Island of What You Know creates a structure that gives you a recognizable form and a
solid identity. You assemble information and create many
stories that define who you are and what the world is, fortifying the framework.

Maybe we have an underlying anxiety about things, but the structure of the Island is designed to help us interpret what is happening in our life so we can feel safe. As long as everything can be explained and then assimilated within the borders of the Island, we do feel safe. It really doesn't matter if our stories make us happy or sad. It doesn't matter if certain points of view work well for us and others do not. The habit of assessing everything through our lens of belief makes the world outside familiar and therefore known.

Unavoidably and without exception parts of your personal construction, the Island of What You Know, fall apart. One example is when a romantic relationship unravels. Imagine that you walk into a restaurant and unexpectedly see the person you love passionately kissing someone else. It's as if the floor beneath you begins to tilt. You become disoriented and it's hard to focus. A piece of what was known has been detonated. It's like getting the breath knocked out of you. You are devastated and it hurts, usually right around the area of the heart. It feels as if your heart has been broken.

Having your heart broken can happen in so many ways. Losing a job. You, or someone close to you, has an accident or becomes ill. Someone you know well dies. You are betrayed and lose trust in something or someone. The breakup of a romantic relationship. Divorce. Bankruptcy. A dream that never comes true. For kids it might be a trip they were looking forward to that never happens, failing a test, a best friend who moves away, an adult who breaks a sacred agreement, or a parent who is distant and lets them down repeatedly.

Being heartbroken begins as a shock and quickly moves into grief, sometimes with intense emotional pain. The pain of grief is largely about our resistance to the unraveling of what is familiar. Our attachment to how things are supposed to be causes great suffering when things fall apart. In effect, the structure we have built collapses. Eventually we adapt—we have to. Somehow we need to function, and we must stop the pain and confusion in order to get back on track. We rebuild with one singular purpose—to stop the suffering. We never, ever want to hurt that way again.

What is interesting is that the emotion that occurs in the moment of the heartbreak is authentic and doesn't lie. Emotions never lie. What you feel is telling you the truth and the truth is always good information. But we don't leave it at that. We react, concocting an agreement with ourselves, assigning meaning to what happened, and then creating a story about it that justifies the agreement.

When everything falls apart, we naturally encounter grief. There are five stages in the process of grief: denial, anger, bargaining, depression, and the last stage—acceptance. When we are heartbroken, the last stage is never completed. It gets bypassed and we form a new relationship with reality, building bigger fortresses along the banks of the island. We manufacture protection. We develop masks to hide behind and find things to act as crutches to help us walk around without so much pain.

Once the island is fortified, we think we are safe but we're not. Whatever it is we devise to protect ourselves sets us up for the next heartbreak. If our personal structure is built to make us safe from the old heartbreak, then it is built on a foundation of sand. What we are so afraid of inevitably happens again. And again. And again. So we rebuild. Each time with a more rigid system of protection than before. But time passes and we forget. What we have created to protect us rolls in like a fog when there is any danger of getting hurt that way again. We don't see that the most recent emotional drama is part of a string of heartbreaks started so long ago.

The First Heartbreak comes when we are children. Small children have an unspoken agreement with their parents. *I can be myself, and you will love me unconditionally. You will protect me, and I'm safe with you. I can trust you, and you will take care of me. I can count on you to be there for me.* Invariably that agreement is broken many times. When a child's world collapses it hurts terribly, so he devises a strategy to adapt. He invents a method to survive without so much pain.

One of my belief-change clients, Cameron, loved to play baseball as a child. His father owned several car dealerships and hardly had any time for Cameron. He frequently criticized Cameron and was hard to please. Cameron was good at baseball and wanted his father to see his performance on the field. Then he'd be pleased! However, his father almost never came to his games. At first, Cameron would watch with nervousness, his attention half on the game and half on the parking lot. This went on game after game. The next year during baseball season Cameron got angry about it. "He's never coming. Forget it. He doesn't care." In later years when his father did come to a game, Cameron was annoyed that he had shown up. "Why is he here? What does *he* want?" Cameron was angry, and as a reaction to his father's pattern of not attending his games, he adopted an attitude of aloofness and arrogance. It was his strategy to never get hurt that way again. Over the years he practiced and perfected it. As an adult, it became a masterful art he used in business and in his personal relationships. His aloofness, arrogance, and anger became his armor, shield, and sword.

Heartbreak strategies are designed to protect us from being hurt in the same way again. One way to do this is to wear a mask. The mask helps us pretend to be someone we are not because we're afraid we will be hurt if we are seen as we are. We develop masks for our parents, for our job, for our friends, and for our lovers because we learned long ago it is not safe to be exposed. We can be arrogant, or we can become invisible. We can smile all the time, being the friendliest person in the world, or we can be harsh with everyone. We may make others wrong to make ourselves right, or find flaws with everyone to justify keeping our distance. We pretend while wearing the mask so we can hide behind it.

The fallout from being brokenhearted is that we devise strategies for protection that prevent us from really living. The passion of living is about taking the risk to connect with life! Living with all that armor dissolves our courage and strangles our passion. When we lose our passion, we find ourselves allowing things to choose us because it is safer than doing the choosing. Revealing our passion becomes too dangerous because we risk what we have invested so much time and energy trying to protect.

The fortress built over time from all the heartbreak is held together with faith. Faith is the glue that binds all the individual beliefs together into the form of "me"—with all its rules and regulations, with all its opinions and points of view. Whenever a portion of our personal world collapses, we develop strategies to protect ourselves. Over the years we cover this ground again and again. We make it stronger each time we use it, and we continually modify the protection to suit the situation. We become wrapped up in what we believe because of our attachment to it. We identify with it. We look for evidence to support it and defend it at every turn. We become the masks we show everyone else. Eventually there is no awareness about what we are doing; it is just an unconscious emotional response triggered when what started as a simple heartbreak is in danger of happening all over again. It is like a spell we are under, an uncontrollable dream that arises and lives our life for us. Over time, the decisions we make when things fall apart become a vault housing a large portion of our faith.

What is really true for you—what is automatic and compelling—is where you have placed your faith. One of the most powerful things influencing any behavior that is making you unhappy is where you have invested your faith, especially in agreements arising from the broken heart. Becoming aware of those agreements and deliberately reshaping them can create extraordinary changes in the way you meet life every day.

Becoming aware of the beliefs born when you were heartbroken provides an immense opportunity to shift your faith. See if you can remember when you had your heart broken from different periods in your life. Go back to each moment. Allow the memory to inform you and notice how you feel. What did you decide about what happened to you? What stopped the pain? What have you created over time that has made you feel safe? When you do those things now, how does it feel?

There is a fork in the road when you encounter the broken heart. There is real opportunity down one path and a narrowing of life itself down the other. When you choose protection, you learn how to shut down, hold back your passion, abandon your dreams, and hide your light. With awareness, the opportunity exists—right now—to expand and step off the Island of What You Know. The grinding to dust of the old structure is a gift, not an excuse to suffer. Recognizing the beliefs born from a broken heart and changing the decisions you made so long ago begins a new journey, releasing your passion and true power.

PART TWO

THE SECOND DREAM

◆ ◆ ◆ ◆ ◆ ◆ ◆ ◆ ◆ ◆ ◆

Our truest life is when we are in dreams awake.
—Henry David Thoreau

CHAPTER 5

THE FIRST STEP: PRACTICE AWARENESS

The posture of awareness is not caught up in the action, but rather observes the action. Its perception is impeccable—watching, feeling, and listening without the Interpreter always explaining what you are seeing right in front of your eyes.

There are four simple steps required to change any belief that is holding you back from the happiness and success in life you dream of. The first and most important step is to sharpen your awareness. The human mind is naturally aware but is so distracted by the Mitote—that relentless conversation in your head dominating your attention—you lose the ability to notice. You lose the ability to notice what has been created by what you believe. You even stop noticing the beliefs themselves. To transform any belief takes awareness. Awareness of what you really believe. In the process of changing a belief, if you can recover your awareness you're almost there. Developing a habit of awareness is most of the task—perhaps 90 percent of the journey. In order to recover your awareness, you must practice awareness.

Awareness is not just about intellectual examination or reflection. An intellectual understanding of your self-limiting beliefs is a good start, but won't take you very far. Being truly aware engages all that you are—emotion, the five physical senses, intuition, spirit, the mind that is always dreaming and . . . your intellect.

So, what is awareness? True awareness is simply perception without judgment.

Recovering your awareness allows you to separate yourself from your habitual point of view so you can observe your point of view. Practicing awareness permits you to become the witness to your own emotional reactions and the stories that emerge from those reactions. This is no easy task. You have a strong sense of "me" and your image is invested there. Up to now all the memories, experiences, stories, and beliefs that populate the Island of What You Know have become the dominant dreamer of your life, interpreting everything that comes into view.

Your Interpreter uses all your knowledge and experiences as a library to extract evidence to support its description. It never rests. It is the narrator, a teller of stories. The Interpreter is not a perceiver because thinking is not a tool of perception. Thinking is a tool of analysis. The Interpreter is the gatekeeper of perception and the more dominant it is, the less awareness you actually have of what is really going on.

It is not possible to practice awareness by allowing the Interpreter to describe and define everything you notice. Using the vantage point of the Interpreter to examine itself is much like having criminals guard the prison. The Interpreter born of The First Dream cannot observe itself with any accuracy because it distorts everything according to your filter of belief.

Practicing awareness requires a whole different approach. Do you remember the book *A Christmas Carol* by Charles Dickens? The main character, Ebenezer Scrooge, is visited on Christmas Eve by three ghosts: the ghost of Christmas past, the ghost of Christmas present, and the ghost of Christmas to come. Over the course of the evening, each ghost takes Scrooge to view himself in a scene from his life. It is as if he is watching himself in a play. The story of *A Christmas Carol* illustrates the perspective of having true awareness of yourself. In the story, Ebenezer Scrooge becomes the observer of his life by standing outside the boundaries of his Island.

Achieving the perspective of awareness of yourself is only possible by becoming the impartial observer of your life; an observer with a specific purpose—hunting. What you are hunting is the expression of any belief that is not serving you. What you are hunting are the limiting beliefs based in old fears that are obstacles keeping you from the happiness and success you desire. When practicing awareness this observer is what I call: *the Hunter of Beliefs*.

Belief is the prey you are hunting. In order to hunt prey you need to learn all about it. It helps to understand its behavior, its habits, and its patterns. Belief is way more than an idea you agree with. Belief is alive and dream-like: a distinct point of view expressing itself through your feelings, behavior, and what you say to yourself and others. In order to be effective, the Hunter of Beliefs needs to learn all about its prey and so is always vigilant, tracking any expression of those beliefs.

There is a posture required to effectively hunt belief. It is very similar to the way the big cats—lions, tigers, jaguars, and cheetahs—hunt. They are intent, intense, and focused. They are acutely aware, always looking for movement—watching with all their senses engaged. Big cats can remain at rest for long periods of time, yet they are ready to explode into action at the sight of prey. They aren't concerned how it happens. If the prey goes left when they expected it to go right, they are not personally offended. They are Masters of Awareness, possessing a certain wisdom—what the Native Americans called animal wisdom. This wisdom is a very useful tool for understanding and practicing awareness.

I have a visualization exercise I give my students. They imagine they are a tiger hunting in the jungle. They dream, while awake, they are perceiving the jungle from this unusual perspective. Slowly and deliberately, they assume the attributes of the tiger: standing on all fours, being covered in fur, having a tail, listening with ears erect, and panting with their mouth slightly open through very large teeth. Rather than approaching the idea of being a hunter as intellectual knowledge, they develop an inner knowing words cannot express. Through active imagination they get an experience of what being the tiger *feels* like.

The posture of the cat is the posture of awareness. The posture of awareness is not caught up in the action, but rather observes the action. Its perception is impeccable—watching, feeling, and listening without the Interpreter explaining what you are seeing right in front of your eyes.

Getting your Interpreter to quiet down is a critical step in recovering your awareness. In the martial arts, as in many of the spiritual traditions from around the world, one of the first tasks given to any new student is to learn to stop the chatter of the mind. This practice has many names. Mindfulness. Meditation. Reflection. The Toltec have a method of ceasing the internal dialog they call "Stopping the World." Stopping the World gives you the unique opportunity to see what's going on without the fog of the Interpreter analyzing everything from the perspective of The First Dream.

Learning to Stop the World builds will. Will is the ability to deliberately decide, with unwavering intent, on a course of action. Strengthening the will allows you to control your attention, produce conscious focused thinking, and decisively choose what to believe.

Stopping the World suspends the Mitote. By stopping your internal dialog you will reclaim a great deal of the energy you normally invest in holding your personal description of the world together. Learning to be still and Stop the World fosters awareness and is a sure step to venturing off the Island of What You Know.

One obstacle that people who attempt meditation face is the idea that all chatter in the mind is bad, must be stopped, and if you can't stop it there is something wrong with you. That point of view actually strengthens the self-defeating beliefs you are trying to change. Rather than an exercise in restraint, I experience Stopping the World as a path to pleasure. What I know is that when I suspend my interpretation, and drop my habitual lens of belief, I experience extraordinary peace. All my problems vanish.

Without the usual story drumming in my head about how things are, what I notice is a new world of vast possibilities.

What creates drama and unhappiness are the wounds in the dreaming mind that fuel fear-based beliefs expressed by the Interpreter. To recognize, change, and heal these wounds requires awareness. By Stopping the World and recovering your will, you'll begin to recover your awareness. Only then can you have any hope of becoming the Hunter of Beliefs, noticing your emotional reactions as they appear rather than being a helpless bystander allowing them to trap your attention.

When we are triggered by an event, strong emotions appear because each facet of the belief system has an emotional point of view. We awaken the giant and the belief casts a spell over us. We become overwhelmed by the emotion, and the perspective of the belief distorts everything we see. The emotion ignites a story and then telling the story ramps up the emotion. Most of the time we're lucky if we even notice it, let alone know where it comes from or know what the belief really is.

An example: Let's say you are in a meeting at work and you have an idea about how to get something done more efficiently. You notice just the thought of speaking about your idea leaves you feeling anxious. When it's your turn to talk and everyone is looking at you, the anxiety gets more intense. In the eye of the Hunter of Beliefs, there is the prey. That rise of anxiety signals the presence of what you are hunting.

When you have moments like that in your life, begin to notice. What story are you telling yourself? How do you feel? What body posture are you holding—bent over and closed in, or upright and open? Has your expression changed? What is the quality of your breathing—slow and deep or fast and shallow?

In the meeting, as anxiety takes over, we may amp up our response. We might blurt out our idea hoping it doesn't get shot down. Our communication style might become defensive. Maybe the tone of our voice becomes softer and our delivery almost apologetic. These kinds of automatic, unconscious behaviors and the underlying emotions can reveal a lot about what we believe.

Hunting prey is about taking the time to stop and notice what is happening inside of your personal dream by using your will to focus your attention. By deliberately focusing your attention, you are practicing awareness. Without awareness, you are not the dreamer of your life but rather the one being dreamed.

When we have moments of emotional reaction things can become unreal almost as if we are navigating through a dream. As the Hunter of Beliefs, the opportunity in those moments is to notice the quality and texture of the dream.

Modern research on dreaming suggests that asleep dreams are not just messages but models of our inner world. While awake, our reason, physical body, and everything around us constitute the frame. During asleep dreaming our body and reason are paralyzed, the solid frame of the world is gone, so our brain builds a model entirely based on our memories, experiences, and beliefs. The essence of this secondary world is very difficult to identify while we are awake in the solid world. One way to understand more of the workings of our inner world is lucid dreaming—having awareness and volition in the asleep dream.

Many ancient cultures practiced the art of lucid dreaming—becoming aware in the asleep dream. For more than 1,000 years Tibetan Buddhists have been practicing lucid dreaming as a means to approach enlightenment. Tibetan Dream Yoga is designed to remind the person striving for enlightenment to constantly recognize that all perception is merely the projection of one's own mind.

The Aborigines of Australia describe the origins and culture of the land and its people as the Dream Time. The Dream Time contains many parts: It is the story of things that have happened, how the universe came to be, how human beings were created, and how the Creator intended humans to function within the cosmos. To them, only extraordinary states of consciousness through the practice of lucid dreaming can help one become aware of the inner dreaming of the Earth and the beings that live there.

The Toltec mythology also describes a lucid dreaming practice. The idea is to remember while you are asleep that you are dreaming. To do this you would practice looking at your hands while awake and ask yourself, "Am I dreaming?" The goal was to remember to look at your hands in the asleep dream, triggering the thought, "I'm dreaming!" If you became aware you were dreaming then you could make choices in the dream. You now had the ability to notice what was going on. You could decide where to go, whom to talk to, and what to do as long as you didn't wake the Interpreter. If you were being chased in a recurring nightmare you could stop running, turn to your pursuer and say, "Who are you? What do you want?" Just that one lucid action could completely transform the dream.

The practice of lucid dreaming makes navigating at will while asleep dreaming possible, but the real benefit is to awaken and recover your awareness in the waking dream. The real point of lucid dreaming is to develop what I like to call *the Art of Lucid Living*.

The Art of Lucid Living is about recovering enough awareness to notice that the simulation you see in your brain is constantly being altered by your beliefs. To notice what you see is really there but modified by the projection of what you believe.

Your mind is dreaming all the time, day and night. To become aware of how your beliefs distort your perception, especially in moments of stress and emotional reaction, remember to look at your hands and say to yourself, "Wait a minute . . . hold on now. . . . What am I dreaming?"

Another way to remind yourself of your commitment to awareness is to get an object—a bracelet, a ring, or a pendant on a chain—and infuse it with the thought, "Wait a minute . . . what am I dreaming?" Use it to trigger certain questions the moment you notice you are getting upset:

- *What just happened here?* (Focus inside yourself rather than making it about others.)

- *How do I feel?* (Pay close attention to your emotions because they never lie.)

- *What am I telling myself? Is what I'm saying to myself absolutely true?*

These are the Questions of Disbelief. Just remembering to ask yourself these questions is a powerful turn of events that allows you to use your awareness and see past the boundaries of your Island. The Questions of Disbelief break the spell of being completely convinced that you are the Interpreter and nothing more.

The practice of Lucid Living and remembering the Questions of Disbelief demand that you become skeptical and stop accepting everything you think as absolutely true. It calls you to notice that most of your stories are made up of interpretation and judgment, not facts. It requires that you stop trusting all the things you profess to believe.

Remembering the Questions of Disbelief and attempting to practice Lucid Living reveals a war. A war for your attention. After years and years of habit, your attention has been captivated by the voice of your thinking. Listen to it and notice what it's saying. *Really* listen to it. If you listen closely it is telling you what you know. Reinforcing it. Discussing it like a lawyer argues a case. The advocate for what you believe. It discusses things like what happened that shouldn't have happened. What you should have done or what they should have done. What you need to do. Why you are right and they are wrong, or why they are right and you are wrong. These points of view are echoed by many voices—the Voices of the First Dream.

The Voices of the First Dream are outlets for the fearful parts of your belief system. It's much like a play. If you had something to say, a commentary about life, you would need a story and characters to express your viewpoint. The Mitote in your mind, your behavior, and the stories you tell yourself about what happened to you are no different. They all serve to express what you believe. Since you are hunting beliefs that are keeping you from being happy, awareness of the expression of those beliefs can be very valuable in helping you make the changes you want in your life.

The Voices of the First Dream are easily recognized. There can be thousands of variations to a few well-defined archetypes, yet their expression is actually very simple. The part of the mind that harbors our wounds is tricky. It thrives on complexity and confusion, yet beliefs based in fear have a common root. Clearing away all that confusion reveals one core belief expressing itself in thousands of ways. *I Can't*, and *I'm Not.*

I'm not good enough. I'm not smart enough. I'm not wanted. I'm not okay as I am. I can't do it right. I can't get what I want . . . and on and on.

I Can't and *I'm Not* can also be projected onto other people. For example, if you expect someone to act in a certain way and they don't meet your expectations, how you react may sound a lot like, "You can't" and "You're not."

The loudest voices of the First Dream are the Judge and the Victim. The Judge comments on how it should be. The Judge says things like, "You're doing it wrong. They're doing it wrong. You should be ashamed. They should be punished. They should act like this. You should act like that." Maybe your Judge is a cagey old man with a long white beard. Perhaps your Judge is the hanging judge from the old American West or is in a white wig scowling behind long black robes. The Judge is the critic and argues from all the rules about what is right and what is wrong. Your rules. Your Book of Rules.

The Judge is the voice of my favorite character in the First Dream: the Demon of Perfection. The Demon of Perfection says no matter what we do, no matter what we achieve, no matter how good it gets, it will never be good enough. This applies to us and is projected to everyone whose image appears in our virtual reality.

Every coin has two sides. On one side of the coin is the Judge and on the other side is the Victim. The Victim says things like, "It's not my fault. No one ever listens to me. It's not fair. I can't help it. No matter what I do, it's never good enough." Maybe your Victim is the parent whose children never listen to their well-meaning advice. Perhaps your Victim is someone whose past has ruined their future, or who is mortally wounded by romantic love. The Victim complains and makes up "poor me" stories because the Victim has no gratitude. Gratitude is a state of being, thankful for all the gifts life offers in the present moment. The Victim is never in the present moment. The Victim looks to the past and believes everything would have been all right *if only*. . . . The Victim looks into the future and believes everything will be all right *when*. . . . It could be all right, but in the mind of the Victim, it never will be.

Another voice of the First Dream is Belle, the saloon girl. The Prostitute. She wants to please everyone and can be anything you need her to be. She's the pretender. This is the voice that will compromise anything to get what we want. What we want is the prize. What we really want is the prize of love and acceptance. Her actions reveal an agreement that says: *I'll do whatever it takes just as long as everyone is happy and okay with me—no matter how I feel.*

Take an inventory. How often do you do something because you think you should or because you feel obligated to? How often do you say yes with your mouth when the rest of you is saying no? What things in your life are you tolerating? Are you tolerating them out of fear, or out of love?

Suppose you are in a relationship and your partner wants to do something you would rather not do. To please them you go along. You say yes, but you're bored and resentful. You wear a smiling mask, but there is something churning underneath. In Spanish the word "mascara" means mask. Belle wears lots of makeup. Lots of mascara. The mask hides why you say yes when you really mean no. The mask conceals the parts of you that you think no one else will accept. The mask hides the truth of how you feel.

Again, every coin has two sides. There is a much more respectable side of Belle. The white knight on the regal horse. The nurse mopping the brow of the wounded. The Rescuer. The Champion. The Hero. They say things like, "Don't worry about me, I'll be all right. I'll fix that for you. Let me do it. I can help you." Because they are two sides of the same coin, the agreements of the hero, the champion and the rescuer are exactly the same as Belle's.

You are more important than I am, and if I do this I'll get what I want. If I act this way I'll get the prize.

The Rescuer—the Champion—the Hero is a voice that reveals *I Can't* and *I'm Not* is a belief that has no respect. The actions of the Rescuer speak loudly saying, *I don't respect you enough to believe you can do it. That's because I don't respect myself enough to believe I can do it either.*

There are many more Voices of the First Dream. They can act defiant, arrogant, aloof, impatient, offended, judgmental, selfish, needy, revengeful, or special—all expressing the same core belief. These are the voices of *I'm Not*. They open channels to express themselves using things like gossip, cursing, comparison, guilt, justification, defending, blaming, complaining, sarcasm, accusation, and lying.

Many beliefs expressed by the Voices of the First Dream have their roots in other people's opinions. Out of habit you interpret what you experience with the information you have gathered. Your knowledge largely consists of what you've learned over time—what you've read, heard, and seen. Much of what makes up your library of accumulated knowledge is actually just other people's opinions—not only the living but your ancestors too. Imagine that. Perhaps 50 percent of the chatter in your mind is a collection of other people's opinions!

So, ask yourself: Is the story of my life really mine, or someone else's?

An opinion is a resilient virus and a powerful influence when it finds a fertile mind. Let's say you are moving into a new neighborhood and the man next door comes over to welcome you. As he is introducing himself, he tells you that the woman across the street is a mean person. The first time you see her you will probably wonder, "Is she really mean?" The seed has been planted.

The actions people take are the result of their opinions. If that action has a big effect on us, then the opinion is contagious—but only if we have a similar distortion of perception. An example: It is well documented that a suicide by a famous person—a celebrity—is soon followed by a wave of copycat actions. Even something as terrible as suicide is merely an opinion that the action is a reasonable solution to a perceived problem.

In addition to opinions we use concepts to support what we believe in an attempt to create a world that makes sense to us. Think about positive concepts—things like goodness, charity, love, service, responsibility, fidelity, honesty, hope, trust, generosity, kindness, wisdom, friendship, and integrity. Do you use these concepts as tools for creating an exceptional life, or do you use them as weapons to make yourself or other people wrong? Take the concept of integrity, for example. If you close your eyes and put the word in front of you, you may get a sense of the meaning beyond what is written in the dictionary. For many it is an emotionally charged word. The word "integrity" can act as a form directing your actions as an expression of personal power. It is also easy to use this word to justify how you or others *should* act. You can use this concept as a way to make yourself right and other people wrong. The hanging Judge can make a pretty good argument about who has integrity and who does not.

A powerful technique to build your awareness is to try and recognize how what you believe is reflected back to you—in your current situation, your conflicts, and by the people you have chosen to spend time with. There is old wisdom that goes something like this: If you want peace, be peace. If you want to attract positive people, be positive. So, how are you being? Take a close look around you and carefully consider the question: *How is all this reflecting what I believe?*

Another way to gain awareness about the beliefs of The First Dream is by watching the coauthors of that dream, the important adults in your life when you were a child. For most of us this was our parents. In The First Dream our parents were merely transferring their worldview to us. They inoculated us with their opinions, reacting to what was outside of them based on their own beliefs.

When we become adults we tend to have a whole list of judgments about our parents and respond to them according to those judgments. We create a series of agreements throughout the relationship, and we experience them through the lens of those agreements.

Consider taking another point of view. If either of your parents is still alive, the next time you are with them, try to see how they process their world. Watch how they react to what comes into their attention. Be the impartial scientific observer watching their behavior and hearing what they say with no judgment.

What do you notice that seems familiar about their behavior? Is it something you do too?

Taking another point of view and developing awareness takes patience, persistence, and perseverance. Recovering your awareness is a process. Just when you think you've got it, another layer reveals itself. There always seems to be more to discover and even more after that.

Unfortunately, most of us want it fixed right now. There is always a rush to solve the problem. If we want to change a belief that is blocking our happiness, the drive is to get to the final step—creating a new belief. To jump to the last step is a mistake, however. The importance of practicing awareness cannot be underestimated.

Normally we solve problems by thinking them through. We use our logic and gather all the information we need from the Island to come up with a solution. In the quest to change a belief, using this method is bound to fail. That's because a belief is a dream projecting itself on everything you experience and so understanding it requires much more than just thinking about it. Awareness of it comes from hunting the dream and tracking its expression and influence in every facet of your life. Discernment comes from becoming the Hunter of Beliefs, practicing the Art of Lucid Living, and asking the Questions of Disbelief. These actions alone will break the spell woven by the belief and start to put you back in the driver's seat.

Once you really understand the agreements you have made with yourself that support your fear-based beliefs—honestly, nakedly, and without deception—then and only then can you have any hope of changing them. Awareness is the tipping point. But becoming aware of what you have agreed to and what that has created can be startling. Many of the beliefs you have are deep and pervasive, and their influence seems to be everywhere. At first it appears to be so complicated you think you'll never get to the bottom of it. There are so many twists and turns. But as you look closer, what seems to be many individual beliefs can stem from one single influence. If it is a belief creating emotional drama that holds you back, most likely it is your particular brand of *I'm Not*.

When you begin to have real awareness about a belief-driven agreement you've made, you get a sense of how prevalent it is in your life. It's like when a rock hits the windshield of a car. At first there is a mark where it impacted the glass, but over time cracks spread out like a spider web across the windshield. You discover that for years you have been supporting and investing yourself in the belief, and now you get caught in the web no matter where you move. The belief has become your all-purpose filter affecting every thought you think, every word you speak, and every action you take. This awareness becomes so overwhelming that you get to the point where you just can't take anymore. You announce, *Enough! I declare independence! I'm starting a revolution!*

Reclaiming your independence is an important step toward recovering your awareness. Becoming truly fed up with an old belief that stands in your way is a good start.

Today, create an inventory of your beliefs, especially ones you recognize as being fearful. Observe, in the best way you can, what you have come to believe, with absolute honesty. Notice when you tell stories about yourself if what you say sounds like the Victim or the Judge. Remember to ask the Questions of Disbelief. Observe if your thoughts are truly yours, or just other people's opinions. These are the first steps to unraveling the enchantment you have been under, breaking the stranglehold of faith, and softening the boundaries of your Island.

Awareness of what you believe opens up a whole universe of possibility. If a limiting belief is based on someone else's opinion, a lie, or a danger of being hurt that no longer exists, and you see that with absolute certainty—the battle is almost over. It is the end of the domination of The First Dream and the dawn of a new beginning. A new beginning of building beliefs that support a life you can love.

CHAPTER 6

THE SECOND STEP: GIVE UP THE NEED TO BE RIGHT

Giving up the need to be right stops every avenue where the belief is expressing itself. It suspends justification and evidence gathering, blocking the primary source of belief-nourishment—YOU!

The second step to changing a belief is letting it go. Releasing it. Freeing yourself from a belief, however, is far more than just an intellectual decision. Liberating yourself from a belief is often not as simple as deciding to disagree. Disengaging from a belief is more than a conclusion that you come to; it's an event with life-changing implications. Letting go of a belief is an act of will requiring that you take a precious jewel that has immeasurable value to you and drop it into the deepest part of the ocean, where it can never be found again.

Deciding you want to break your belief-based agreements is a necessary step, but if you absolutely want to change the core belief it can't be done by thinking or affirmation alone. Remember, belief is not born of words but experience, and what we decide the experience means.

The attachment to what you believe is often way too strong to be broken just by saying to yourself, "I'm done with this. I want to stop." Obsessive or addictive behavior like overeating or smoking is rarely changed by putting a sign on your refrigerator stating, *I'm thin,* or *I'm smoke free.* Your behavior is an expression of your beliefs and cannot be changed simply by changing your mind.

Letting go of something is a lot like true forgiveness. Consider the act of forgiveness. Are there people whom you have not forgiven? Are there things you have done that you have not forgiven yourself for? Why not?

Often, we just can't forgive. Although we may want to completely let it go, the debate in our minds and the emotion tied to the event are too strong, especially when the offense has occurred repeatedly over a long period of time. Our insistence on the arguments that support our position become a jewel of immeasurable value. The attachment is very powerful, much like the tale of Gollum from the book trilogy *The Lord of the Rings,* and his addiction to his "precious"—the One Ring.

Listen to the discussion in your mind when you don't forgive, when you just can't let it go. It's all about what you did and what they did. Who should have done this or who should have done that. Who's right and who's wrong. It sounds like an argument. It sounds like a lawyer arguing a case.

When lawyers come before the judge to plead a case, they provide evidence, cite precedent, and present an argument with one specific goal in mind. They are there to prove they are right. If you listen to what you say to yourself when you think about someone you can't forgive, what you hear is an argument about being right. You can't forgive because you can't let go of the conviction that you are right.

The reason you can't let go of what you have come to believe—even if it is making you unhappy, even if you now strongly disagree—is because you are the champion of that point of view and will defend it at every turn. You need to be right.

Many times old wounds live on long after those who caused them have passed away. Why? Because we take over. We nourish the wound, care for it, and even embellish it. The point of the belief thrives because we are right about it.

Have you ever listened to someone complain that what they really want is impossible to achieve? If you listen closely to what they are saying, they will present all sorts of evidence to prove their point. If you suggest another way of looking at it they will likely respond, "Yes, I hear what you are saying . . . but." The *yes, . . . but* indicates they are addicted to their need to be right.

In order to let go of an agreement you have made that has been reinforced thousands of times—that has your attention, hooks your mind with its point of view, and has an emotional perspective that is overwhelming—give up the need to be right. Giving up the need to be right stops every avenue where the belief is expressing itself. It suspends justification and evidence gathering, blocking the primary source of belief-nourishment—YOU!

Deciding to give up the need to be right is not just a thought but a far-reaching action that releases your investment of faith. Faith in what you believe.

Giving up the need to be right does not mean what you observe isn't accurate. You just give up your interpretation, because that's where the attachment is to being right.

As an example, suppose you see a homeless man on the street. He appears to be sick and doesn't seem to have much energy. His clothes are torn and tattered. He looks dirty, as if he hasn't bathed in a long time. In your mind you may start to think about how you might help him. Maybe you can even save him from whatever has gotten him to this place. Perhaps you start thinking about how this person is lazy, and if he just got a job like everyone else he wouldn't have to live on the street. Maybe you are disgusted by anyone who would let themselves get into such sorry shape.

What you notice about the homeless man and the condition he's in is most likely correct. The rest is your assessment, your interpretation. Whether you are going to be the hero, the social worker, the reformer, or the judge is all about the need to be right.

Giving up being right starts by noticing the habit of needing to be right. Being right often appears as: defending, justifying, acting offended, incensed, or outraged. Intolerance, arguing, applying semantics to your arguments, condemning, being overly critical, acting condescending, sarcastic, or being addicted to accuracy are typical behaviors of being right.

Have you ever gone over and over in your mind how someone has offended you, arguing to yourself why they are wrong and you are right, and when you finally confront them you are overwhelmed by a powerful emotion?

Emotional energy feeds your limiting beliefs, and a sure way to manufacture that food is by being right about your story.

Everybody defends their point of view. Nobody likes to be wrong. So why give up your need to be right? It's such an integral part of our culture. We are trained from a young age to be right. Being right is a way to be accepted. Being right is a way to avoid the sting of criticism. Being right is a way to win. Editorials; call-in shows; courtroom battles; terrorism; debates in coffee shops, classrooms, and the bedroom all touch on the need to be right. Perhaps you could try to convince yourself that you should give up your need to be right because of some moral argument about forgiveness or because it sounds like a reasonable thing to do. For me, there is only one good reason to give up the need to be right. Because it feels good.

Years ago I went on a trip to the Inca ruins at Machu Picchu in Peru with don Miguel. One day he asked me, "Why am I here?"

I thought about it and I said, "To teach us."

"Nope," he replied. "Wrong answer."

I thought about it some more and said, "To change the world."

"Nope," he replied. "Wrong answer."

He was in a particularly feisty mood that day and although I had several clever answers come into my mind, part of me knew I was still headed in the wrong direction.

"Okay," I said, "tell me. Why are you here?"

"For pleasure," he replied.

It took me a very long time to understand what he meant. At first, I thought it was about physical pleasure, like getting a massage or lounging in a hot tub and sipping fine wine.

What I began to understand was that he deliberately acted in certain ways because of the emotion it invoked—because it felt pleasurable to him. He loved to play, laugh, and have fun. No matter what kind of exchange I had with him, there was always a sense he was meeting me with kindness, respect, and love without conditions. So I tried it too. The emotion tied to treating myself and others with respect, kindness, and compassion was highly pleasurable. Learning to Stop the World, turning off my mind and riding moment to moment in a sensation of feelings with no words to describe it, was delightful. Merging with nature, breathing it in and allowing it to infuse me, was exquisite. I learned that when I aligned my will with the creative power of pure being, and gave up being accurate, I felt tremendous pleasure.

When you can't forgive someone for an offense the simple fact is that you are using them to abuse yourself. Being right and being upset only hurt you. Thus the most compelling reason to give up the need to be right is pleasure. If you take the time to notice how you feel when you take any action, without using words to define your perception, you may discover that your emotions provide invaluable advice based on how you feel.

If you are struggling to give up a belief, give up the need to be right about it. When you do, your attachment to the belief you want to change will crumble, igniting an emotion that is simply delightful.

To stop feeding an old belief that is no longer serving you, give up the need to be right.

CHAPTER 7

THE THIRD STEP: LOVE YOURSELF WITHOUT LIMITS

Change as an act of self-love is a pledge to treat yourself with compassion rather than criticism, kindness rather than self-loathing, and extreme care rather than self-abuse.

The third step in changing any self-defeating belief requires that you treat yourself with love. *Real love.* Real love is simply love without limits—love without any conditions at all. Treating yourself with real love is accepting yourself, as you are right now, despite any conversation in your mind about how you should be, shouldn't be, or what you should have done in the past.

The notion of unconditional love was something I heard about many times before I ever stopped to consider it seriously. When I finally did, I thought: *It's impossible!* I was repelled by people who I thought were acting badly. They made me uncomfortable. And, I was embarrassed when I acted badly. For many years I could never accept myself, or anyone else for that matter, without a long list of conditions.

Most of us know about love with conditions. We can love if the right conditions are met, and if we love, then we expect something back. Love with conditions is an agreement that implies, *I can accept you, but only if you act in a certain way. I will love you if . . . .* Within that agreement it is safe to love. It applies not only to everyone around you, but to the way you treat yourself as well.

In the First Dream we learned what love is. When you were a child, did you ever make a giant mess, or break something expensive, and your parents were upset? Perhaps they said things like: *Look at what you have done! Why can't you be more careful? What's wrong with you?* They were angry and it was your fault. You did something wrong and now they didn't seem to love you like before.

In a situation like that, we decide it's up to us to make it better. We need to be different and dream up strategies to get them to accept us again. Or maybe we react, angry at them for their reaction. *It was an accident. I didn't do anything wrong. I can't understand why they are so upset with me. What's* their *problem?* We become so agitated by their behavior that we decide they need to be different before we can love them again.

These two responses arise from exactly the same agreement. It just depends whether we have a predilection for pointing the finger inwardly at ourselves or outwardly toward everyone else.

Childhood dramas around things like breaking something valuable happen thousands of times in hundreds of different ways on the Path to Now. We learn we are not okay as we are, or decide they are not okay as they are. We learn that giving and getting love are a game—a game of punishment and reward.

The rules of the game demand that when you do something wrong you are guilty, you need to be punished, and you will have to beg for forgiveness. When you are a "good girl" or a "good boy," you get the prize—the prize of love and acceptance.

In the First Dream, there are two basic rules about getting or giving love:

- Love and acceptance are commodities that exist outside of me, and to get them I have to say the right thing, do the right thing, and be the right thing.

- I am responsible for others' emotions and happiness, and in turn, they are responsible for mine. If they react in a negative way to something I do or say, I need to change my behavior so they will be happy and accept me. However, if they do or say something that upsets me then it's their fault, and they need to behave in a different way before I can be happy and accept them.

As we become adults the Voices of the First Dream use this definition of love from our Book of Rules to judge everyone, including ourselves. The Book of Rules defines the unbendable standard of how you should act and how you should feel. Perhaps your Book of Rules says: *Certain emotions, like anger, are not okay.* If so, then when you become upset you might think: *I shouldn't act this way. I shouldn't feel this way. I need to fix it.*

So to fix it, you embark on the path of self-improvement. But often the motive for self-improvement rests on one simple belief laced with agreements like:

+ I'm not okay as I am.

+ No one will accept me like this.

+ I can't accept myself like this.

Buying into the myth of self-improvement is a protective story we tell ourselves to feel better—a thin veneer easily torn by distress, disappointment, or the perception of failure. At its core the myth of self-improvement is self-rejection because its seed is the belief, *I'm Not . . .*

We are unhappy in the present moment because we are not the way we should be. Happiness lies somewhere in the future—*it will be okay when . . .* Or, happiness is irrevocably lost in the past—*it would be okay if only . . .*

What we reject is our shadow-self peering through a thick lens of fear-based beliefs. Largely hidden our deepest beliefs form what we perceive as indisputable reality—a viewpoint far more powerful than what we pretend is true.

As we embark on the path to self-improvement it's no wonder we reject ourselves. Our self-made program is infected by a virus—the Parasite of Fear—and in conflict with whom we have decided we should be. When it comes to our unacceptable parts, we want to hide them, lock them away, pretend they don't exist, "transform" them, or annihilate them out of existence.

Of course you want to banish the behaviors you're embarrassed about. They *abuse* you! Out-of-control emotions result in out-of-control behavior. And it all starts with the Mitote in your mind fabricating all the little stories you tell yourself. If those stories are fueled by beliefs based in fear, they ignite emotions that have little basis in reality.

Let me explain: Imagine you are walking on a mountain trail, and all of a sudden a violent thunderstorm boils up and lightning is striking all around you. Your body would likely feel fear because there is a real and present danger. Makes sense, right? But what if there is a situation where no real danger of injury to your body exists? Can fear emotions still be provoked? You bet! And it all begins in the mind. Let's say someone criticizes you at work (in your view without justification). In your mind you begin to tell yourself a story defending yourself. The story will explain why either you're not a "bad" person or they are a "bad" person. Either way, the story creates the perception that there was an attack. As a result your emotions will respond perfectly—as if there is real danger—even if there is no actual threat.

Once you have awareness about what your fear-based beliefs create, it makes perfect sense that you want to change what is holding you back from experiencing true happiness. It makes perfect sense that you want to change what makes you suffer. But let me ask you this: *If you fix what you've discovered so far on your path to self-improvement, is that it? Will you be truly happy?* Not likely. That's because there are many sides of you that you have yet to discover—integral parts that you still reject. Each time you uncover another "undesirable" part of yourself, the whole process of trying to change it, so you can finally accept yourself, will start again.

When I was a teenager I had a volatile relationship with my stepfather after my mother died. I flatly rejected everything about him. My brother and I would make fun of him and mock him behind his back. When I left home at 16 years old, I thought that I had erased him from my life forever. But as I got older I noticed many of his mannerisms leaking out of my own behavior. I was horrified!

Like it or not you are a product of the people you spent large periods of time with. Their behaviors, actions, and words shape you, not always by conscious agreement, but by long association. You may dismiss them, but they are invisibly intertwined within you *for life*.

Conflict with the things we cannot abide in ourselves is rejection of ourselves. Looking down or looking away is how we hide our fear from others at the same time hiding it from ourselves. Banished, our wild, dark side becomes neglected and abused. In times of great stress it seeps out in the most inappropriate moments—because it will not be ignored. Hidden and segregated, this part of us becomes more volatile and powerful. Only awareness, full acknowledgement, and self-compassion will weaken that power. Only love without limits will take that power away.

In order to practice love without limits, you need to recognize what real love is. There are over thirty words in the English language alone related to the concept of love. And most of them have to do with romantic love. Is your notion of romantic love really love? And how does the sentiment of love apply outside of romance, like loving your family, your community, your work, and most importantly, yourself?

The concept of love from The First Dream is not love at all. It's fear.

Because love is so hard to pin down with words and can be confusing to apply, the easiest way to recognize it is to understand what it is not. What love is not is something we are infinitely familiar with and can identify with no misunderstanding. Fear. Not the fear that keeps you from getting hurt physically, not the natural response to real danger, but unreasonable fear. Fear that makes you suffer. Fear based on lies.

The simplest definition of love is not-fear. In just the same way, fear based on a lie is not-love.

There is a simple litmus test. In whatever situation you are in, no matter what decision you need to make, listen to the dialog you have around it. Examine all your internal arguments and points of view. Ask yourself this one simple question. Is this fear, or is this not-fear?

Love is a powerful perspective that can be applied to everything in your life. Moment to moment, day in and day out. Understanding love without limits doesn't take a lot of effort or intellectual prowess. Love without limits is simply the act of taking a point of view that serves only one master. Not-fear.

What is really true is that in every moment of your life you have done the best you could. As much as the Demon of Perfection argues to the contrary, it is not possible that in the moments that have passed you could have done any better. You get it when you get it. You realize something the minute you realize it and not one minute before.

After you awaken and have awareness about your beliefs, cultivating the point of view— *I should have known better. I should have realized this years ago! How could I have wasted so much time?*— is about needing to be right. Hashing it over and over in your mind, obsessing about what has happened and what you *should* have done keeps you stuck in the role of defender of the *I'm Not* belief despite your intent to change it.

If you are dedicated to ongoing growth, self-improvement, and your own personal excellence, then saying, "I did the best I could at the time" is not an excuse, but recognition that the Demon of Perfection is a liar. If you want to be happy and learn from the actions that haven't given you the results and sense of well-being you desire, being overly critical of yourself and vowing to banish the "bad" parts of yourself won't help and actually support the agreements you are trying to break.

Loving yourself without limits is about taking care of yourself the same way you would take care of someone you love deeply—your beloved. Loving yourself without limits is treating yourself with the kind of love a mother gives her little ones, regardless of the mischief they have gotten into that day.

Loving yourself without limits requires being impeccable with yourself. Being impeccable doesn't mean that your behavior is without flaw. Rather, being impeccable with yourself simply means that you choose not to take any action or support any point of view that creates unnecessary suffering. Worry is a perfect example of a behavior that is not impeccable. When you worry, what problem does it solve? How does it make you feel? Vowing to be impeccable with yourself is a powerful personal agreement, a pledge to make a choice to refrain from any action or interpretation that is harmful to you. This one simple agreement will forever eliminate worry, self-judgment, and regret.

Today, write a confession. "I am . . ." and list all your flaws. Include the things you know about, the accusations others have made that you can't quite accept, the things you barely will admit to yourself, and the things you deeply regret. Making this list may not be pleasant because these are the unacceptable parts of yourself. Now, what if you view the changes you'd like to make from your list as self-love rather than self-rejection? What if you view the changes you'd like to make as a gift to yourself rather than a condition that must be met before you can accept yourself? When we look in the mirror and want to lose weight it's common to think: *You look terrible! When are you going to get some willpower?* Instead try: *I'm going to lose this weight because I respect myself and I am going to do what is best for me.* Change as an act of self-love is a decision to be impeccable with yourself, a pledge to treat yourself with compassion rather than criticism, kindness rather than self-loathing, and extreme care rather than self-abuse.

Love in The First Dream is love for a reason. *I will love you if . . . I will love you when . . .* Love without limits has no reasons. In the end loving yourself without limits is a decision you make based simply on the way it feels.

When you discover an agreement you made that now seems foolish to you, it is normal to feel like a fool. No matter what it is you have created for yourself, you have done the best you could up to this point. Give up punishing yourself because you should have known better. Stop rejecting yourself because the emotions tied to what you have come to believe don't allow you to behave the way you'd like to. Give up the need to be right about how you think you should have been in the past, or where your development needs to be today. As you learn to practice awareness, learn to practice kindness. Treat yourself with kindness, respect, and love without limits when considering all the decisions you have made up till now—even the foolish ones.

Each step in changing a belief ties into the next one. Changing a belief starts by becoming acutely aware of it opening up the real possibility of making a different choice. Next, changing a limiting belief is about giving up your need to be right—withdrawing the energy that nourishes the belief. Finally, changing a self-punishing belief like: *I'm Not* requires that you agree to never go against yourself, releasing your attachment to the idea that you have to make serious changes before you can ever accept yourself.

Imagine, for just a moment, that you have no fear of judgment from others. That you just don't care. Not the fear-based *I don't care*, but the detachment that comes from not needing love from outside of yourself. Now, close your eyes. Envision yourself floating, warm, safe, and spilling over with boundless joy.

What I thought was impossible—love without conditions—is absolutely possible! I can see now that the idea that I could only accept myself when I accomplished my long list of "improvements" was a trap I could never escape from. I can see now that the "bad" parts of me that I was embarrassed about have provided pathways to understand how to be truly happy every day. I can see now that the most effective motivation to achieve change is *I love myself*, rather than *I'll love myself when I change*.

So take the oath to be impeccable with yourself, and treat every part of you (even the parts you don't like) with acceptance, kindness, and respect no matter what. And like magic, you will dissolve any limiting belief you want to change.

CHAPTER 8

THE FOURTH STEP: CREATE A NEW DREAM

Now that you understand what you have come to believe, and have chosen to stop feeding any beliefs that are not serving you, you are ready to accept new beliefs that support the happiness you desire.

The first three steps to change a belief will help you recognize and stop nourishing any belief that isn't serving you. The fourth step is about taking action to create a new belief—or reconstruct a belief you want to change—and that can only be done by using the same elements that created it in the first place.

Like all animals, we possess the natural elements of perception: the physical senses of sight, taste, touch, hearing, and smell; as well as the focus and discernment of our awareness—our attention. A complement to the human intellect, the elements of perception are an integral part of the integrity of every human being. It is through these elements that we observe the world, and assemble our unique filter of beliefs.

Your personal belief system, designed in The First Dream, was constructed by choosing where to focus your attention, establishing channels of communication through the elements of perception, and making agreements by investing your faith over time. Your interpretation of what you experienced through your filter of beliefs created your version of what is real—the Island of What You Know.

There are billions of human beings on the planet, each with their own unique virtual reality. Strong opinions about how we should act are lodged in ideologies about government, religion, economics, spirituality, and so much more. We are bombarded by media—radio, TV, print, and the Internet—all vying for our attention. Every group, whether it be a country, a town, a corporation, trade organization, or the family next door, has a distinct point of view that is apparent when we are in the sphere of their influence. Each person, each group, contributes to the collective mind that is dreaming through their particular flavor of beliefs. Each time we focus our attention on any portion of that dream, we plug into whatever is being communicated. By allowing our attention to be hooked we consume whatever is being broadcast.

In every moment, aware or not, you decide where to assemble your attention. Moment to moment you put your attention on something—an object, a sound, a picture, someone talking, or a thought. Wherever you place your attention a channel of communication is opened and meaning is received. When you establish a channel of communication with your attention, your beliefs distort the input, and at the same time what comes through the channel is inexorably modifying your personal dream of life.

These are the dynamics of the First Dream: allowing your attention to be captivated, agreeing with other people's opinions, and hardening your beliefs by fabricating stories and insisting you are right about your stories. Clearly noticing the dynamics of the First Dream and having real awareness of what you have agreed to believe begins what the Toltec called "The Dream of the Second Attention." For simplicity I will call it *The Second Dream*. When you intend to change a belief you consciously direct the focus of your awareness—your attention—for a second time.

In The First Dream your beliefs are in full control of your attention. In The Second Dream your attention begins to control your beliefs.

In order to begin to assemble The Second Dream, you choose, for a second time, where to place your attention and what to believe. Now that you understand what you have come to believe, and have chosen to stop feeding any beliefs that are not serving you, you are ready to accept new beliefs that support the happiness you desire.

The fourth step to changing a limiting belief starts with rewriting that belief. If you have uncovered a belief that leaves you feeling unhappy, unwanted, or unacceptable, change the language you would use to describe that belief so that it reflects your new declaration.

It is very important to understand that the language you use to describe a belief is *not* the belief itself. It's the way that you communicate to your mind and other human minds. Belief is more than words. Much more. For just a moment, close your eyes and find the point of reference for the old belief you want to change. It has a particular point of view. It's a dream with a familiar overpowering feeling born of experience that you understand perfectly *without language*. But to begin to change a belief start with the mind, and what you intend to do. Begin by rewriting the belief you want to change. Agreements are born of belief so after you rescript the belief, choose a few new agreements that rework the old belief you want to modify.

One of my belief-change clients, Cate, had a pattern of being focused on doing everything just right. Before she went to meetings at work, she would rehearse in her mind all the possible conversations that might occur so she would be sure to say the right thing at the right moment. She would go to parties and try to blend in with whatever was happening in the room, but shortly after she arrived she felt like she didn't fit in. Dating was a disaster because she was so focused on her performance being perfect it was impossible for Cate to relax and be herself.

Cate had come to me with the specific goal of jump-starting her career. But that was a smoke screen. From my vantage point it was easy to see how her pattern of behavior was holding her back, not only at her job, but in everything she did.

As a result of our work, Cate became aware of a hidden belief driving her behavior. Through the opinions of the adults that had been impressed upon her in The First Dream, she had agreed to the idea that no one would accept her just the way she was. She discovered she had adopted the first rule of getting love: *Love and acceptance are a commodity that exists outside of me. To get it, I have to say the right thing, do the right thing, and be the right thing.*

She was so afraid she would get it wrong, it almost paralyzed her. Her pattern of trying to do everything perfectly was a mask covering intense anxiety. She had an overwhelming fear of being found out because what she really believed was that there was something terribly wrong with her, and there wasn't any way she would ever get it right.

To change her *I'm Not* limiting belief Cate started by mapping out some new agreements she could make with herself: *First, I agree that the approval, acceptance, and love I want begin with me. I will no longer take personally people's opinions about who I am or what I should do—it's their dream. I agree to be impeccable with myself and never go against myself. I have many goals I have yet to achieve, and I want to improve going forward, but in this moment I accept myself just as I am.*

Identifying your new belief, and the agreements that support it, is a powerful first step. If you are not clear about what you want to achieve, you will never achieve it. Write it down! This may sound simple, but real transformation begins when an idea is written down on paper. Until you write it down, it's merely a thought that may evaporate as easily as your night dreams do when you wake up in the morning.

Next, find a way to keep the task in your consciousness and begin to practice it. Remember that you have, over a long period of time and through lots of effort, mastered the belief you are trying to change. There is a very old saying: *Practice makes the master.* To master anything, practice it!

I live in the Rocky Mountains of Colorado and each winter I try to improve my skiing technique. The truth is I learned to ski without lessons and so I have lots of bad habits. I love watching skiers who come down the mountain effortlessly with seemingly perfect form. It's inspiring but also frustrating because I'm still trying to remember all the little nuances of technique and on occasion I struggle to execute the simplest things. When I talk about my process to people who ski well, I hear the same thing over and over again. It takes time and practice before old habits change. Like skiing, belief-change is a practice sport.

Belief does not change overnight, but rather a new agreement gains momentum each time you choose it. In The First Dream, what you believe controls your attention. Your beliefs have power because you bestowed them with power. In just the same way, each time you invest yourself in a new belief the balance of power shifts. Each time you take action and choose a new agreement you have made, the domination of the old viewpoint will recede.

The next thing you can do to reinforce a belief is create a new story and gather evidence to support that story.

Little children talk themselves to sleep making up stories to help organize the events, actions, and feelings of each day. As young as two, they use storytelling to explain what is happening to them. Storytelling is a natural part of our development resulting in the beliefs, oaths, and promises that later dominate our thinking.

Everybody tells stories to themselves that support their beliefs. The book you are reading right now is just a story, my story. But without awareness we are deceived by the narrator of the story which debates the rightness and wrongness of everything.

Today, with awareness, rewrite the story you have been telling. Clean it of all judgment and fear. Design a story that will never hurt you. Add new elements that enhance it like forgiveness, patience, compassion, and acceptance. To redesign any belief, drop the old story, tell a different story, and assemble evidence that strengthens your new story. Up to now you have been very successful establishing that your old story is correct by defending it and gathering evidence to prove you are right. If you want to adopt beliefs that support happiness and nurture a new dream of life, start by telling a different story that supports those beliefs.

Once you have recovered your faith through the Questions of Disbelief, reinvest your faith in a new belief. Evidence gathering is a powerful way to do that. Use this dynamic to sustain beliefs that foster happiness and personal excellence rather than a device to create drama. You learned long ago to gather evidence so that you could prove you are right. Now, make evidence gathering your ally. If one of the self-limiting beliefs you have discovered is: *I can't ever do it right*, notice and catalogue when you get praise for your performance. Recognize how you feel when something turns out exceptionally well. Make a habit of honoring and accentuating all the events that support what you are trying to create. Start collecting different evidence.

Another great way to strengthen a new belief is to imagine its perspective. Close your eyes and *dream it*. Because we are a product of what we experience, you'd expect that to begin to believe something you have to experience it over and over again. For example, to become a skilled tennis player you need a lot of experience playing tennis and succeeding at it. But is that all? No. First, you have to decide you are capable of it. In some way you have to agree you can fully embody what you want to believe even if it isn't true . . . yet.

Have you ever heard the story of the four-minute mile? For many years people believed it was impossible for any human being to run a mile in less than four minutes. Roger Bannister, an English physician and middle distance runner, broke the four-minute barrier in May of 1954. Bannister believed it was possible, imagined it, and used his knowledge as a physician to his advantage. He painstakingly researched the mechanical aspects of running and developed scientific training methods to aid him in achieving his goal.

Within one year after Bannister shattered the belief barrier, 37 runners broke the four-minute mark. The year after that, 300 other runners did the very same thing. We become capable of achieving anything the moment we decide it's possible.

For years, athletes have used visualization techniques to enhance their performance. They imagine themselves performing well at their sport repeatedly as if they are dreaming it. To a well-conditioned, well-trained athlete, belief is an important key to exceptional performance. To take on a new belief you don't have to wait until you experience it as a solid part of your life. You can begin to step into the perspective of the belief *before* it becomes a habit. If you understand the results you want and the emotional texture of your new belief, then you can dream it deliberately. If you can dream it and know how it feels as a point of reference, then, in that moment, you can embrace the perspective of the belief you are trying to manifest.

Working on the steps to change her belief, Cate wrote down her new agreements and began to collect evidence to support them. In order to collect evidence, she reviewed her memory and wrote down all the moments she could remember where she had the experience of being loved, appreciated, self-confident, and secure. She started there and used that as a point of reference. A point of reference, in this case, is just a memory that has an emotion attached to it creating a particular point of view. If you know how it feels, you can find your way back.

Next, she used the technique of imagining the perspective of the new belief. In order for her to use these memories as a point of reference, I instructed her to close her eyes and remember—to sense, to feel, and to dream. She imagined moments where she had the experience of being loved, appreciated, self-confident, and secure until she could really feel it. She visualized this until it was real for her. In her imagination she took this new point of view into the memory of being at a party where she was uncomfortable and struggling to be liked. She dreamed, while awake, being at the party with her new way of being—her new belief.

The next time she was in a situation that triggered the perspective of her old belief, she used her awareness to notice how she was feeling and perceiving. Because she had identified, practiced, and dreamed the perspective of the new belief, she now had the opportunity to choose something else to believe.

Another way to support your new agreements is to seek out someone who has real faith in the belief you want to adopt. Find a mentor for your new belief. Look for someone who is living, day to day, the point of view you want to create for yourself. An association with a belief mentor does not always have to be a one-to-one relationship. You can find the influence of mentors in books, movies, seminars, or articles. Whether they are famous or live just around the corner, their actions and accomplishments speak volumes about what they believe.

Using the posture learned by becoming the Hunter of Beliefs, experience how they move through the world influenced by the belief you want for yourself. Maybe the life you've only dreamed of exists outside of the Island of What You Know, but it surely exists inside someone's Island. If you want to begin to experience the things you want, that are not true for you right now, venture off your Island.

When I started my own belief-change process I hit a wall. I thought: I *can't do this. I have been living like this my whole life and it will NEVER change.* But during my time with don Miguel I could see what I was telling myself was a lie, an old story I kept alive by feeding it. He was the perfect mentor for me because he clearly didn't believe those things. And, he would repeat over and over (part affectionate insult and part inspiration), "If I can do it, you can do it. And if *you* can do it . . . ANYBODY can do it!"

When you directly experience the life-dream of people who believe what you'd like to believe, you will receive a simple but startling revelation—It *is* possible. Because if they can do it, you can do it too.

Changing a belief takes time so be patient and kind to yourself. Imagine that you own a house but rent it out and let someone else manage it for you. One day you get a call from the property manager letting you know that the neighbors are complaining about the people renting your house. When you go to check it out you find there are some pretty rough characters living there. The property is a mess. You tell your renters they must change their behavior or they will have to move out. A month later the neighbors call to complain again. When you go back to investigate, you find nothing has changed and so you ask your renters to leave. You tell them you cannot agree to them living in your house any longer. They finally move out, but when you go back to inspect the house, you discover it's still a mess.

Changing an old belief is a lot like that. At first, you really don't know what is going on. When you begin to gain awareness you negotiate with yourself hoping you don't have to make any big changes. Finally, on the day you stop tolerating the situation you'll say to the belief that has been residing with you for so long, *Get out of my house and take your stuff with you!* But even after the agreements supported by the belief are broken, there is still a lot of debris left by years of investment in the belief. It takes time and effort to put your house back in order. But that's not all. It takes courage, commitment, and desire.

When Cate went to a party after designing her new agreements she had the goal of walking up to people she didn't know, being at ease, and starting up a conversation. She tried it but noticed the old script still running in her head. Although she wanted to give up after the first few times, she didn't back down. That's because she had the courage to change.

To have courage doesn't mean you don't have fear. The act of courage confronts and acknowledges fear. To have courage means to persist despite the fear. Embracing what challenges you means that your dedication to the goal is more important than protecting the fortress you have constructed—that the freedom is far more important than comfort. To have courage requires that you detach from any story about what might happen if you do this, or do that, and willingly step away from your safety zone—the Island of What You Know.

If Cate went to the party, tried to connect with a stranger, and succumbed to the old script of needing acceptance, that would be an act of agreement. Agreement with the old belief. By pushing past the fear, her action, because of her courage, was now an act of deliberate disagreement. Her disagreement was an act of disobedience and restored her authority. Before, she had abdicated her authority to the old belief, capitulated, and bowed down to the fear.

To change a belief and step past the boundaries of the Island requires not only courage, but a commitment to be impeccable with yourself. But what is a commitment—the act of keeping your word? Saying you will do something and then doing it? It's more than that. True commitment is a Yes—not just a sound that comes from your mouth, but a complete promise that comes from the heart, the mind, and the spirit. True commitment is a resounding Yes that radiates from every fiber of your being.

Changing beliefs and breaking old agreements is a process that takes you beyond the borders of the Island of What You Know. To make the journey requires passing through the Gates of Change. The Gates of Change are where you meet the wall of your own fear and encounter resistance to pushing past what you know. To pass cleanly through the Gates of Change requires an unwavering commitment to yourself. It requires a Yes.

Many times when we are asked for a commitment we say yes with our mouth, but what we really mean is no or maybe. Have you ever been served in a restaurant, or at the checkout counter, by someone who never looks you in the eye and just goes through the motions? Have you ever watched a couple in a relationship where they seem to ignore each other and rarely connect except to argue? Most likely they are showing up and pretending to honor the commitment that they have made but saying no with almost every part of their being. You can see it. You can feel it. When you say yes but don't mean it, you throttle the flow of possibility and stand frozen at the Gates of Change.

Sometimes what stops Yes is the idea that saying yes has a high cost because we will be committed for a very long time. We think saying yes means we will be trapped, so we ride the fence with no more than a maybe. A true Yes is an impeccable action in the moment. Yes has no time frame. Whatever action you decide to take, no matter how routine, say Yes now. In the next moment, you can say no, with awareness and no fear, if that is what you choose.

Yes with all your will begets passion and authority. Real authority, not the cheap authority of someone who believes

I'm Not telling someone else, *You're Not.* Yes is an act of faith, throws open the Gates of Change, and supercharges the act of creation.

Yes is a choice made with recognition that the exact result is an unknown. You can still say Yes, understanding that you can't control everything, you can't predict everything, and you can't know with any certainty exactly what will happen next.

Finally, Yes aligns with desire. Dissatisfaction with a fear-based belief has an important purpose, but burning desire moves mountains. Every act of creation starts with desire. Deep desire is a maneuver brimming with passion and accelerates the process of change.

To reweave the fabric of your beliefs come to the Gates of Change, consider what you want, and if you choose to walk through, say Yes. Start on the journey even though you don't know where it is going to take you. See what happens when you choose to believe something else. Cultivate your desire, have courage, make a commitment, say Yes and take action!

You have always agreed what to believe. And perhaps, without knowing it, you have been using the power of belief against yourself. Starting today, apply that power consciously, creatively, carefully, and constructively. With awareness choose to believe what brings you pleasure, peace, power, purpose, and passion. When you change what you believe, your behavior changes. When you change what you believe, you change what you do. If you want to experience lasting, enduring change, create a new dream for the rest of your life. A new dream fueled by the power of belief!

CHAPTER 9

THE PROMISE OF ACCOUNTABILITY

Your intent is the mastery of your faith. Whether you are aware of it or not, by your faith you have gotten everything you have really asked for. You have invested your faith by agreement and now that is what you truly believe.

Every word in every language is nothing more than an agreement. If I say, "I adore my cat," you understand what I have said only because we agree on the meaning of the sounds. What we may not agree on is the emotional charge of certain words. For instance, if you love cats then the word "cat" will invoke a pleasant emotional response in you. If you dislike cats then it will invoke an unpleasant emotional response. How you feel when you hear a word depends on if you relate that word to what you love or what you fear.

When I work with groups of people I frequently ask, "What do you feel when you hear the word, *responsibility?*" Without hesitation, they say things like:

It feels like a lead blanket covering me.

I feel like I'm about to be blamed for something I did.

A feeling of dread comes over me because I have to do something I would never choose to do.

In fact, only a few people in each group have a positive interpretation of the word, "responsibility."

As children we learn what a word means, and how to apply its meaning by observing the adults who raised us. If they had the opinion that being accountable was taking the blame, being punished for what you did wrong, or slogging through life doing what *responsible* people do, then we will too.

Perhaps you recognize this point of view. I know I do. It was once my favorite story. It's a story that interprets responsibility from the perspective of being a victim. Being a victim was my true purpose in life. I deeply desired peace and happiness, but I complained about everything. I blamed other people for the way I felt. I blamed my circumstances for my troubles. I was disappointed in myself and convinced I was in mortal combat with forces inside of me—a victim struggling against things I could never change. But later, when I began to recover my awareness, I realized that to have such a struggle meant there must be at least two (if not more) of me, inside me! And there was. The Creation and the Creator—the Dream and the Dreamer. In a bit of pure insanity I had been battling against what I had chosen, designed, and agreed to.

In the belief-change process there is a line in the sand— a point beyond which you cannot pass until you make one reality-shattering decision. Fail to cross that line and you will be forever stuck, vaguely aware of your limiting beliefs and unable to change them. Cross that line and you will experience a world far beyond your Island, a world brimming with unending promise and possibility.

How can you cross the line? It's simple . . . but I warn you . . . it's not easy. It's not easy because there are no excuses, there are no exceptions, and there are no bargains to be made—ever! Here is the naked truth. Ready?

To cross the line you must become fully accountable for every one of your thoughts, decisions, actions, and beliefs.

To change what you have created requires awareness, honesty, and accountability. In order to modify anything that's become a habit, you need to become accountable for your part in creating it in the first place.

How you have processed everything that has happened to you and the agreements you have made as a result was entirely based on choice. Things don't always go the way you want them to and sometimes they don't go well at all, but the decisions you make in those moments are what you have agreed to believe.

We think we are in control of so many things, but in fact we are not. All we have control over is where we place our attention and the decisions we make about what happens to us, or around us. We decide what things mean and those meanings become the stories we tell about everything.

If we are truly accountable for the stories we make up about how things are, and how we are, then we are not victims. As children, we are innocent and dependent. The adults are bigger, smarter, and stronger. There is no question about that, but the story of the victim is that they had no choice. Victim self-talk: *It's not my fault; it's not fair; I can't help it*; is based on the point of view that it happened to me and I am powerless to change it, even now. If that is true, there is no hope at all . . . but it's not true.

There is hope, and it is in the Promise of Accountability. No matter what has happened to you, in your reaction to it you decided what it meant, made agreements, and fabricated a story to support those agreements. At each juncture, you made a decision. Mindful or not, you said yes to a certain point of view.

Perhaps you have read about, or even know personally, someone who was in an accident and is now in a wheelchair paralyzed from the waist down. Some people who have had this happen to them live a life of bitterness and anger. Others take on the challenge and find a new dedication to expressing their joy and gratitude for life. What happens to us is often out of our control, but we alone agree what to believe about it.

Up to now you have devoted an enormous amount of energy constructing your own personal version of what is true. You have created a story about how things are and each time you retell it, you invest your faith in it. But many times we don't recognize that the story we tell acts to abuse us. We don't notice that we frequently take on the role of the Victim. However, if we listen closely, any trace of complaining indicates the Victim is speaking. For the Victim, their story supports the place where they are stuck. *I can't. It's hopeless. I don't have any other choice. It's out of my control. I don't know what to do. It's her fault, it's his fault, it's their fault.*

If you want to know where you have invested your faith, listen to the stories you tell yourself and anyone who will listen. What is interesting is all the little details of the story that prove you are right are not that important. What is important is the belief behind it.

One spring I was in Austria teaching a belief-change seminar and I had set up some private appointments. I had a session with a woman who only spoke German, so the interview was conducted with an interpreter present. The plan was that each person would speak a few sentences and then pause so the interpreter could translate. The woman was in her early fifties, nicely dressed, her brown hair pulled back in a bun, and she had a pleasant smile.

She came in and said, "Everything is all right with me, but my husband thought it would be a good idea if I saw you." I asked her, "What can I do for you? What do you want?" She ignored the question and talked about her husband and his problems. I asked her again, "What do you want?" She stared at me with a puzzled look on her face, and again talked about her husband's problems. I asked her the same question a third time. "What do *you* want?" She started to cry and began talking very quickly, barely pausing to take a breath. My interpreter stopped translating because she couldn't keep up.

I didn't understand what was being said, but I could see what was going on. Her facial expressions, her body language, and the tone and volume of her voice said it all. She was in her story. She launched into her justification of why she was stuck, he needed to change, and how it would never get better until he did. It wasn't important that I knew what the sounds coming out of her mouth meant. It was the point of view of her story that was significant. She was a victim. Her story supported the belief that she was hopelessly trapped. Her investment of faith declared: *This is the way it is and until he changes there is no way out.*

Your intent is the mastery of your faith. Whether you are aware of it or not, by your faith you have gotten everything you have really asked for. You have invested your faith by agreement and now that is what you truly believe.

The Promise of Accountability says you have come to where you are today because you decided what it all meant. You have come to where you are today because you agreed what to believe. You have come to where you are because you alone invested your faith. The Promise of Accountability is about recognizing all the actions you have taken to create and nurture the beliefs that are now obstacles to pursuing the happiness you desire.

The Promise of Accountability is good news and refutes the voice that states—*This is the way it is and there is no way out.* If beliefs are created by focusing your attention, agreeing with other people's opinions, deciding what things mean, fabricating stories, and collecting evidence so that you are right about your stories, then there is no reason why you can't employ all of those strategies to build new beliefs—this time with awareness and a clear intent.

Now that you have been presented with the four steps to change a belief: *Practice Awareness, Give Up the Need to be Right, Love Yourself Without Limits,* and *Create a New Dream,* I offer one final instruction: Change your relationship with that emotionally charged word, "responsibility." Embrace it for it is the foundation of your creative power. You have always had the power to choose something else.

Something else to believe. If you want to experience lasting change then become accountable for all the agreements you have made up to now, and reinvest your faith deliberately in beliefs that empower you. Cross the line and embrace full responsibility as the creator of the life-dream you are living. Just this one decision will make all the difference in the world.

CHAPTER 10

I AM

The real you—I AM—is your own inner fountain of love,
inspiration, power and joy.

The most powerful beliefs you can choose are the ones
that rest on a solid foundation. The firmest foundation of all is the truth. The truth is that the belief, *I'm Not* is
a lie. Before we ever agree to believe *I'm Not* it was someone
else's opinion and probably someone else's opinion before
that.

If you believe you are small and insignificant, or that
you don't deserve abundance, or that you will never realize
your most precious dreams, then you agree—*I'm Not*. If
you play roles and wear masks to protect yourself so you
can't be seen, then you agree—*I'm Not*. If you accept the
notion that persistent sadness about the past or constant
anxiety about the future is normal, then you agree—*I'm
Not*. Regardless of your accomplishments, if you capitulate
to a life of little joy and don't believe you can ever achieve
success in the full circle of living, then you agree—*I'm Not*.

Consider for a moment—if you eliminated from your
thinking: anger about the past, worrying about the future,

taking things personally, making assumptions, assembling judgments, and having expectations of others—what would be left? Not much I suspect. You see, when you Stop the World, even for just a moment, drama in your life vanishes—like magic! What creates unhappiness is not what is, but what you believe it is.

Regardless of what you have allowed yourself to believe, your authentic Self shines like a bright star. It's always there and never goes out—an endless source of all things divine. An unlimited wellspring of delight and creativity. It's life itself. YOU are life itself. You and everyone who takes a breath are intimately connected to all living things and that which created them. Through this connection anything is possible. The real you—*I AM*—is your own inner fountain of love, inspiration, power, and joy.

Beyond the world created by what we believe, we are not separate from anything. We are a part of everything and everything is a part of us. The entire universe and everything in it are one presence that has magically and magnificently projected itself into billions of forms. Each of us is one of those forms and in the same moment the entire universe. To quote a well-worn cliché, you are a drop of water and at the same time the whole ocean. But we focus our attention on the drop, forgetting the ocean. In an act of magnificent self-importance we define ourselves by our image, our story, and the pressure of our daily lives. Because of what we agree to believe, we can't see past our Island, yet at the deepest level we are unbounded.

Your beliefs form an interpretation system—a system that allows you to navigate the world you think you know.

But in the place of pure Being all of your beliefs and stories fall away, except one—*I AM*.

You are LIFE experiencing itself through the human body, perception, thought, and emotion. You are the art of the creator. You are *I AM*.

The Voices of the First Dream—the Judge, the Victim, and the Prostitute—are teachers that lead us to I AM. Once redeemed, the Victim teaches us about our own personal power and authority. The Judge teaches us about justice and truth tempered by love. The Prostitute teaches us about self-love, respect, and faith. Each voice of The First Dream confronted becomes an ally.

When you allow the story you tell about yourself and everything around you to collapse—in that moment everything is all right as it is. Once the road of *I'm Not* is no longer tended, natural forces will heave the road. Withdrawing your investment of faith in *I'm Not* reveals what is, without effort. *I AM*.

I AM okay. *I AM* good enough. *I AM* capable. *I AM* in this moment, perfect. *I AM* peace. *I AM* able to love myself without limits. *I AM* human. *I AM* Divine, as is all the creation I see around me.

Allowing yourself to invest your faith in *I AM* reveals the true power of belief.

You are *I AM*.

PART THREE

TOOLS

FOUR STEPS TO CHANGE
ANY LIMITING BELIEF

THE FIRST STEP

Practice Awareness

To transform any belief takes awareness. Awareness of what you really believe. In the process of changing a belief, mastering awareness is most of the task—perhaps 90 percent of the journey. Reclaiming your awareness opens a universe of possibility; a new beginning of choosing beliefs that support a life you can love. In order to recover your awareness, practice awareness.

In Order to
Practice Awareness

Map out the Island of What You Know

◆ ◆ ◆

Track your reactions as the Hunter of Beliefs

◆ ◆ ◆

Recognize the Voices of the First Dream

◆ ◆ ◆

Ask the Questions of Disbelief

◆ ◆ ◆

Identify the Interpreter

THE SECOND STEP

Give Up the Need to Be Right

To let go of any belief that no longer serves you, give up the need to be right. Giving up the need to be right suspends justification and evidence gathering, blocking the primary source of belief-nourishment—You! Giving up the need to be right is a far-reaching action releasing your investment of faith. Faith in what you believe.

In Order to Give Up
the Need to Be Right

Use awareness to notice
when you need to be right

❖ ❖ ❖

Observe what being right creates

❖ ❖ ❖

Stop collecting evidence

❖ ❖ ❖

Give up the addiction to accuracy
and allow your feelings to guide you

THE THIRD STEP

Love Yourself without Limits

Change as an act of self-love is a pledge to treat yourself with compassion rather than criticism, kindness rather than self-loathing, and extreme care rather than self-abuse.

In Order to
Master the Third Step

Accept the "unacceptable" parts of yourself.

◆ ◆ ◆

Reject love according to the First Dream

◆ ◆ ◆

Embrace the act of forgiveness

◆ ◆ ◆

Banish the Demon of Perfection

◆ ◆ ◆

Be impeccable with yourself

THE FOURTH STEP

Create a New Dream

After you have awareness of what you have come to believe, and suspend nourishment of the beliefs that are holding you back, design new beliefs that support the happiness you desire. This step can only be accomplished by using the same elements that created the old system of beliefs in the first place.

In Order to
Master the Fourth Step

Rewrite the belief you want to change.

◆ ◆ ◆

Rewrite your story, practice it,
and gather evidence to support it

◆ ◆ ◆

Imagine the perspective of
the new belief and dream it!

◆ ◆ ◆

Find a belief-mentor (someone who
believes what you'd like to believe)

◆ ◆ ◆

Charge through the
Gates of Change with a Yes!

DEFINITIONS

Attention
The focus of your awareness.

Awareness
Perception without judgment.

Belief
A belief is a dream, a simulated reality shaped by your most pivotal experiences and what you have decided those experiences mean. A conviction that exists beyond language, belief projects its point of view onto all that you perceive, distorting what is.

Hunter of Beliefs
Tracks the expression of any belief that limits your happiness and keeps you from pursuing the life you desire.

I AM
I AM is an endless source of all things divine. The real you—an expression intimately connected to all living things and that which created it. An infinite inner fountain of love, inspiration, power, and joy.

I'm Not

A belief passed down from the authors of The First Dream that you are not okay as you are, you are not enough, and no matter what, you never will be. *I'm Not* implies that you are not adequate, and to get love and acceptance you have to say the right thing, do the right thing, and be the right thing.

Island of What You Know

Your own personal island of safety constructed of your beliefs, other people's opinions, all your accumulated knowledge, and experiences. It is the result of what you have agreed to and invested your faith in. It is the container of "me" bounded by what you believe.

The Art of Lucid Living

The art of becoming aware, while you are awake, that you are dreaming and that your beliefs are modifying the dream, distorting what you perceive.

Mitote (me-toe-tay)

The runaway chatter of the mind—our incessant internal dialog. Refers to the cacophony of characters in your head, a riot of opinions, a thousand voices in the marketplace all talking but none listening.

Promise of Accountability

All you have control over is where you place your attention and the decisions you make about what happens to you, or around you. The Promise of Accountability says you have come to where you are because you agreed and thus invested your faith. You have always had the power to choose something else. Something else to believe.

Questions of Disbelief

Not completely accepting everything you think, everything you say, or what anyone else says. Asking the Questions of Disbelief—*What just happened here? How do I feel? What am I telling myself? Is what I'm saying to myself absolutely true?*—breaks the spell of being completely convinced that you are the Interpreter living on the Island of What You Know and nothing more.

The Book of Rules

The law your inner judge uses to pass judgment on you and everyone else around you. The Book of Rules is your book of judgment.

The Broken Heart

Unavoidably and without exception certain parts of your personal structure—the Island of What You Know—fall apart. What has become your foundation shifts, causing what you have built to collapse. Eventually you adapt because you have to. You need to function and so you develop strategies to avoid pain and make you safe again. You rebuild, this time making your structure of belief more rigid to protect you, but at the same time keeping you from living openly with real passion.

The Demon of Perfection
This character from the First Dream speaks with the voice of the Judge: "No matter what you do, no matter what you achieve, no matter how good it gets, it will never be good enough." This applies to you and is projected to everyone whose image appears in your virtual reality.

The First Dream
In order to pass information onto us when we were children, the adults who raised us needed to capture our attention. In this way they taught us language. Once we understood the code, they could tell us about everything they assumed, expected, knew and believed. This process of hooking our attention for the first time creates, by agreement, our initial dream of how the world is.

The First Heartbreak
Small children have a natural unspoken agreement with their parents—*I can be myself, and you will love me unconditionally. You will protect me, and I'm safe with you. I can trust you, and you will take care of me. I can count on you to be there for me.* Invariably that agreement is broken many times.

The Gates of Change
Changing beliefs and breaking old agreements are a process that takes you past the borders of your comfort zone—the Island of What You Know. To make the journey requires passing through the Gates of Change. The Gates of Change

are where you meet the wall of your own fear and encounter resistance to pushing past what you know.

The Interpreter
Uses all your accumulated knowledge and experience as a library to find evidence to support its personal description of the world. A teller of stories, the gatekeeper of perception, the narrator of your beliefs.

The Second Dream
Awakening to what you have agreed to believe begins The Second Dream. When you intend to change a belief developed in The First Dream, you focus your awareness—your attention—for the second time, choosing what to believe. In The First Dream your beliefs control your attention. In The Second Dream your attention begins to control your beliefs.

Toltec
An ancient culture that thrived in what is now the pyramid ruins of Teotihuacán in the high midlands of Mexico. In a tradition that dates back thousands of years and continues today, the Toltec were known throughout Mexico as men and women of knowledge. The Toltec philosophy claims that there is no way for us to change unless we have an understanding of how we create our own unique perception of the world. Their description of human awareness is that the mind never rests, and one of its main purposes is to dream. They concluded we are dreaming twenty-four hours

a day, and what we experience inside our personal dream is significantly altered by our beliefs about everything.

Voices of the First Dream

The Voices of the First Dream are outlets for beliefs that define the Island of What You Know. These inner voices expressing beliefs born from fear belong to various archetypal personalities including the Judge, the Victim, the Prostitute, the Hero, the Rescuer, and many more—all expressing a common theme.

Yes

Yes is an impeccable commitment. Not just a sound that comes from your mouth, but a total promise that comes from the heart, the mind, and the spirit. Yes carries authority and passion. Yes throws open the Gates of Change and supercharges the act of creation.

STOP THE WORLD

Each day rushes on with more to do than there is time to do it. A perpetual merry-go-round that never stops so you can get off. What would happen if you suddenly stopped the world—even for just a few moments? Better yet, what would happen if you stopped your personal interpretation of everything, allowing yourself to observe the world without your habitual lens of belief? What you might see is a new world of possibility without the story. Your story.

To stop the world is to practice awareness, and for just a moment, surrender your description of everything that keeps your attention occupied.

Sit someplace quietly where there isn't anyone around to disturb you. Somewhere you feel safe. Take off your shoes. Sit up straight. Don't cross your legs. Rest your hands on your thighs. Get comfortable and then don't move! When you shift your body, you give in to the mind which is competing for your attention.

Your inner dialog—the *Mitote*—has your attention much of the time and so when you sit down to be still, there will be a war for your attention. Your mind will suggest that you fidget, scratch, or get up and write a note about something you might forget. To strengthen your will, don't move at all.

Just breathe. Slowly. Follow your breath with your attention. Breathe in through your nose slowly, imagining you are pulling air in from all over your body. Breathe out through your mouth, making the sound of the ocean or the wind. The in-breath is the will deliberately directing your attention as choice. The out-breath is letting go. Releasing everything.

As you breathe in let your body expand. As you breathe out let your awareness expand. Notice how you feel, in your emotions and in your body. Resist the temptation to describe this to yourself in words. Just be aware with no attempt to define it or explain it.

Start by practicing 15 minutes each day, several times a week. Exercise this new habit. If you lose your attention to the chatter in your mind, don't make yourself wrong. Just refocus. Find the space between the thoughts. Be kind to yourself. There is no such thing as doing it right.

ACKNOWLEDGMENTS

To my beloved Susan Marshall and Noah Dodd, whose love, support, and belief in me have been the greatest gift of all.

My heartfelt gratitude to all my teachers. There have been so many over the years I can't recall everyone. To the teachers who were in my life for a while and to those who only crossed my path for a moment in time, I thank you. Without any limit to my appreciation for his hand in my transformation, I thank don Miguel Ruiz, M.D.. In addition, I wish to thank Gini Gentry (La Doña), Rita Rivera, Barbara Emrys, Allan Hardman, Victoria Allen, and Luis Molinar for their guidance.

A special thanks to Miguel Ruiz, Jr. for his enthusiasm, and to Simeon Hein for inspiring me to keep going.

Another special thanks to Caroline Pincus and all the wonderful folks at Red Wheel Weiser, and Bob Friedman at Hampton Roads Publishing for their vision and patience in bringing this all together.

Finally, my love and gratitude to all those who have supported this work over the years and who were each, in some way, instrumental in developing the ideas found in this book. A partial list includes: Maru Ahumada, Alison Barrows, Suzanne Bastear, Beverly Beniot, Lanex Brink, Maggie Caffery, Fred Dearborn, David Dibble, Mitchell Dozor,

Samie Dozor, Hal Foreman, Ed Fox, Thomas Gruner, Kim Gustafson, C. J. Hall, Marianne Heindl, Judy Herreid, Simeon Hein, Ron Jones, Camille King, Donna Krebs, Kit Kyle, Dawn Link, Christine Magdalene, Brad Meyers, Colleen Miller, Thomas Miller, Brandt Morgan, Darryl Morgan, Cynthia Morris, Sabine Mueller, Dr. Gene Nathan, Wendy Newman, Robin Nicolaus, Jeff Offsanko, Emily Palko, Massimo Perucchini, Peggy Raess, Susyn Reeve, Stewart Sallo, Eric Sanderson, Birgit Schwarz, Barbara Simon, Sandy Shipp, Shelly Steig, Joanna Strang, Mark Wergin, and Teresa Wergin.

ABOUT THE AUTHOR

 In 1996, after a chance meeting at the pyramids ruins in Teotihuacán, Mexico, Ray Dodd embarked on a 6-year apprenticeship with don Miguel Ruiz M.D. (author of the best-selling book, *The Four Agreements*). Now an expert in the process of changing beliefs, Ray helps individuals and organizations shift limiting beliefs in order to create lasting and positive change. Prior to beginning his belief-change work, Ray had careers as a professional musician, engineer, and a corporate executive for a nationwide facilities company with over one billion dollars in annual sales. Today, he is a much sought after speaker and teaches seminars about his signature Power of Belief ™ programs throughout the United States and abroad.

BELIEFWORKS

Focusing on changing what you do—changing your behavior—often results in short-term improvements that ultimately don't last. The problem? It's simple. When you only address the behavior you want to change by deciding to do something different, you ignore what is driving that behavior. If you want to achieve lasting change you also need to change what you believe.

BeliefWorks is an organization dedicated to assisting individuals and organizations in identifying core beliefs that stand in the way of their goals, hopes and dreams. Once any self-limiting beliefs are identified, using our signature Power of Belief™ process, we facilitate the integration of a new framework of empowering agreements, helping you successfully achieve the changes you want to make . . . changes that last!

Please visit our website: *www.beliefworks.com:*

- ◆ For information about our Power of Belief™ programs

- ◆ To find out how to order companion guides for this book

- ◆ To book Ray Dodd for media events, or to speak at your next public event, association conference, or corporate meeting

Hampton Roads Publishing Company
. . . for the evolving human spirit

Hampton Roads Publishing Company publishes books on a variety of subjects, including spirituality, health, and other related topics.

For a copy of our latest trade catalog, call (978) 465-0504 or visit our distributor's website at *www.redwheelweiser.com*. You can also sign up for our newsletter and special offers by going to *www.redwheelweiser.com/newsletter/*.